With My Song I Will Praise Him

With My Song I Will Praise Him

Claude H. Rhea

BROADMAN PRESS *4 463*
Nashville, Tennessee

JACKET PHOTOS: JOE NICHOLS

Subject heading: RHEA, CLAUDE H.
Dewey Decimal Classification: B
Library of Congress Catalog Card Number: 76-17946
Printed in the United States of America

DEDICATION . . . This book is
dedicated to my wife Carolyn who
has been my unwavering middle C
for twenty-five years

FOREWORD

Those who hear Claude H. Rhea sing are deeply moved not only by the beauty of his voice and the excellence of his technical performance but by a remarkable spiritual quality of depth, sincerity, and love. A deep commitment to the will of God in his life is the secret of the assurance and poise with which he meets whatever life brings.

As music consultant for the Foreign Mission Board of the Southern Baptist Convention, his travels took him to many parts of the world where his testimony in song and spoken word brought inspiration to large congregations in concerts, evangelistic crusades, and conferences.

His deep commitment to missions has continued as a strong motivating factor as he has served admirably as dean of the School of Music at Samford University.

WITH MY SONG I WILL PRAISE HIM is a welcome volume which will bring delight to hosts of old friends and will introduce others to a remarkable Christian whom to know is to receive a personal blessing.

BAKER JAMES CAUTHEN

PRELUDE . . . The Fine Art of Gifting

"Carolyn, I have a *marvelous* gift for you!" my husband excitedly exclaimed. "You'll never guess what it is!"

No, I probably *couldn't* guess what my husband was "gifting" me with, for giving unique gifts has always been one of his unique talents!

During our twenty-five years of marriage, we have "exchanged" gifts many times. For example, there was the *bell!* For years Claude had yearned for an authentic farm bell. Finally he found one while singing in South Carolina one November and promptly purchased it for *my* Christmas present! Never having yearned for a farm bell myself, I couldn't fully appreciate it; so it became the perfect gift for me to give *Claude* the following Valentine's Day! Graciously he accepted it; proudly he mounted it in our Texas backyard; exuberantly he rang it to call the children home or to celebrate special occasions.

Then there was the bell *tree!* During his travels abroad, Claude had collected as souvenirs miniature bells from various countries. Now he needed a live, custom-tailored tree out in the yard, where he could hang his bells so they would ring in the wind. A bell tree, he decided, would be an ideal gift for *my* forthcoming birthday! So tinkling bells, tickled by a Texas breeze, heralded my day! Four months later, his own birthday provided an appropriate occasion to "exchange gifts" again and to present him officially with his own bell tree!

The procession of unusual gifts from my husband began in Florida shortly after our wedding. Impulsively, Claude bid on a beautiful silver service at a jewelry store auction. His was the highest bid; and, though almost penniless, we two graduate students became the proud owners of that gleaming symbol of culture! (As a matter of fact, Claude borrowed the money from the bank, anticipating that he could repay it shortly thereafter with the honorarium from a forthcoming revival meeting.) Through the years we have enjoyed the luxury of gracious entertaining with a silver service we might never have owned had he waited for the time we could really *afford* it!

The years that followed in New Orleans added additional gifts. Claude purchased an antique pump organ, which he discovered while singing in Kentucky; and he acquired a bargain grandfather clock on Canal Street there in the "Crescent City." Though originally purchased as gifts for me, they became my gifts to him in our typical transfer-of-ownership pattern of gifting.

The Spanish bagpipe he brought me from a trip to Europe was the beginning of his musical instrument collection from around the world. His first attempt to play it on our back porch was hysterical! Hearing the strange sounds that issued forth, our neighbor's Simamese cats, caged in her backyard, stampeded! Their terrified cries mingled with the weird squeals of the bagpipe!

Christmas in Virginia some years later brought me a matched pair of dainty, hand-carved Guatemalan midwife chairs. Angry feelings surfaced as I peeked into the bamboo bags which held the strange assortment of unassembled pieces and recalled how I had hinted so often that I wanted an electric waffle iron for Christmas!

The chairs were only one of Claude's many unusual gifts for me which he collected during his travels around the world: a spear and shield from Africa, mola from the San Blas Islands, a blue butterfly tray from Brazil, an original painting of a cock fight from Indonesia, brass candlesticks four-feet tall from Thailand. Strangely enough, many of Claude's "impractical" gifts have now become treasured heirlooms; and I would willingly sacrifice, if necessary, in order to keep them. The lovely organ peals out heartwarming hymns and joyous Christmas music. The grandfather clock contains our family history etched inside its door. Various items from the "Rhea Museum of Fine Arts and Ends" are vital elements in the decor of almost every room. Claude's unique gifts through the years are distilled memories of our life together: agreements and disagreements, adventures and misadventures, joys and heartaches, victories and failures, achievements and dreams.

But I treasure his *intangible* gifts even more than these *tangible* ones. Somehow Claude has always felt that the gift of growing a finer self is a special kind of gift to the one with whom life is shared intimately. So interspersed throughout the years have been such gifts to me as his creating an original composition by setting a favorite poem of mine to music, taking art lessons in watercoloring, struggling with harp lessons (unsuccessfully), making his first record album, compiling a cookbook, writing music to children's songs. His own intangible gifts of the spirit inspired me in turn occasionally to gift him likewise: the courage to learn to drive after my sister's death in an automobile accident; the audacity to write poetry and children's songs and devotional books, the nerve to cook some exotic dishes, the strength to become a college coed again for teacher certification. This gifting process has stretched me in areas I might never have dared explore otherwise!

Other intangible gifts of the spirit—laughter, music, in-spiration, joy—which he has given through the years, have added deeper dimensions to my life. (Claude asserts that a coconut hit him on the head that summer while we were student missionaries in Hawaii and that I captured him while he was knocked out!) His spontaneous gift of humor has leavened many of life's flat fiascos.

His gift of music has been an *outlet* for tension and worry, an *inlet* for joy and trust. Set to music, our twenty-five years of marriage would range from children's merry melodies to profound religious oratorios.

Frequently, his gift of inspiration has caused me to reach even higher. He has ignited a spark of inspiration in other lives too, those whom he has touched through his many roles: father, son, son-in-law, friend, deacon, preacher, educator, musician, administrator.

According to Teilhard de Chardin, "Joy is the most infallible sign of the presence of God." If this is true, then my husband is a living example of one who abides in the presence of God. His gift of joy, even in difficult circum-stances, keeps spilling over! His own contagious optimism about the *goodness of life,* the *goodness of people,* and the *goodness of God* is one of his greatest gifts!

Proudly I present to you my husband: CLAUDE RHEA, A.B., B.Mus.Ed., M.Mus.Ed., Ed.D., F.R.S.A.,* D.O.C., R.E.V., D.A.D., J.O.Y.!

CAROLYN RHEA

* Fellow Royal Society of Arts

GRACE NOTES

This is a book about God's continuous, amazing patience and his never-failing love toward one of his children. As the recounter of the deeply personal experiences shared on the following pages, I am a fellow onlooker with you, the reader. It's what God has chosen to channel through me which makes the retelling of the pilgrimage intriguing. An ever-present, all-wise, all-loving God is not in the puppet manufacturing business. He does not choose to manipulate any of us in a whimsical, high-handed manner. Rather, he makes each one of us in his own image—liberated to true selfhood—free to love and laugh and hurt. Each of us is awesomely different—yet strangely similar in the common ventures of shared humanity. Each growing and changing person, when honestly facing the demands of his own life, perennially stands in need of God's redemptive pruning, refreshing watering, nourishing, harvesting, and cyclic replanting.

It's our distinctively human milieu to be surprised by joy, to be tempered by totally unexpected adversity, and to be strengthened and supported in our utter dependency by God's unfailing, undying love. The struggle is inevitable for each one of us. The appropriation of God's custom-tailored "grace gifts" awaits.

That's what this story is all about. Like your pilgrimage, mine is open-ended—it's in the process of being written. Because Christ lives, I dare share with you (1) how by

15

grace he's brought me safe thus far and (2) why my antici-
pation of days as yet unlived are so full of potential. Indeed,
each one of us can commit our personal history to him
with an unswerving conviction and assurance which says,
"I faith you, God!"

CLAUDE H. RHEA
Birmingham, Alabama

CONTENTS

1 The Lord Is My Strength

"The Lord is my defense and my shield; my heart trusted in Him, and I am helped. Therefore my heart rejoices and with my song I will praise Him" (Ps. 28:7, Berkeley).

I shall never forget that eventful October day in New Orleans. Tensely, I sat across the big mahogany desk from a world-renowned internist. Slowly, and with detachment he pronounced those dread words which one instinctively feels will always happen to someone else—but never to oneself personally. "Son," he said, "you have cancer." Terse, unblinkingly, and without emotion, he spoke those factual words which with unbelievable swiftness brought my puny little world crashing down in ruins at my feet.

"The X rays confirm my diagnosis," he continued. "Come. Let me show you." He wearily arose. His noncommittal expressions reflected long years of playing games with death. Ponderously he walked across the room and flipped on a fluorescent light behind the X-ray viewer. My inmost parts were made public, eerily outlined in silvery barium. "This white spot about the size of a crab apple in your right side is the cancer," he said. "It's on the cecum. These streaks seem to indicate that it's metastasized, that is, spread. It doesn't look good at all. You'll need immediate surgery—tomorrow! I suggest you choose a surgeon right now. Any questions?"

Questions? Questions? How could I frame questions in a mind which was gripped by the icy reality of the words I had just heard from the doctor? I was shattered. Incredulous. Unnerved. Aghast. Unbelieving. I arranged for a surgeon and then, trance-like, moved from the cool, antiseptic climate of the doctor's office out into a bright autumn afternoon.

The outside world moved in what seemed to be carefree abandon, uncaring and unaware of my private anguish. Instinctively I climbed under the steering wheel of my ancient push-button vintage Rambler station wagon. I inserted the key, turned it, and after the traditional pause felt a majority of the six cylinders shudder to reluctant life. Moving along the broad avenues of the "Crescent City" I wound my way through and around innumerable five o'clock traffic crises to the sanctuary of the seminary campus. How strangely beautiful this island of quietness seemed in the midst of the rushing, pushing mobs of homeward-bound workers. Once again I reflected how very much I enjoyed my ministry of teaching in that place.

The dreaded moment was rapidly approaching. I wheeled onto Seminary Place and then into my driveway. How could I tell my wife Carolyn and our children the news? How does a man share his deepest agony with his dearest ones? Slowly I climbed from the car and went toward them. My family was raking leaves. The beautiful scene burned itself deeply into my memory. Joyous family togetherness. My children frolicked in piles of raked-up, tree-abandoned leaves, throwing them like lazy, weightless javelins at nonexistent enemies.

Carolyn looked up, caught my eye, and read my plight even before I could utter a word. With the sixth sense of a wife, she already seemed to know. Wordlessly, she came to me and hand-in-hand, we slipped quietly into our bedroom. Closing the door, we fell to our knees, crying our hearts out to God. At that moment in time, I felt as Elijah must have felt in that long ago . . . abandoned . . . stricken . . . "the heavens were as brass." Prayers seemed to stop at the ceiling.

After a few hours, a certain sanity-preserving numbness began to possess me. The nightmare would not dissolve into a new scene. It was unshakable reality. Details must be faced—even if mechanically. Family must be contacted, churches notified, praying friends enlisted. Life moved inexorably onward.

Later that evening I phoned our longtime friend and confidant Baker James Cauthen, executive secretary of the Southern Baptist Foreign Mission Board. As I tried to put into words my sense of questioning and initial analysis of the situation, he provided a sympathetic sounding board. Even by long-distance phone I caught the intensity of his interest and compassionate concern. "Next week is Missionary Day at the Seminary," I said. "Carolyn and I *were* planning to make public our decision to volunteer for appointment as overseas missionaries. But now on the very brink of this momentous vocational change the door has closed. The here and now of cancer shatters this long-cherished missions dream. Will you pray for us, Dr. Cauthen?" I requested.

This gracious, powerful man of God quietly and simply said, "Yes, Claude, I will." It was only months later that I learned the extent of his simple pledge to me. For immediately he cabled missionary "prayer-warriors" around the world. Within a matter of hours there was a far-flung intercessory prayer meeting going on—one which encircled the entire globe.

I slept fitfully that night, tossing and turning, mulling over the traumatic events of the day, consciously and subliminally reexperiencing agonies both real and imagined. Mercifully, sleep came in the early morning grayness.

When I awoke to a new day, there was a different dimension. Something was happening. I was experiencing a new process. I was on the *receiving* end of intercessory prayer! My wife Carolyn captured the essence of this moment in a poem from one of her books, *My Heart Kneels, Too.*

"The Invisible See Saw"

I felt that someone prayed for me,
For there came an inner awareness
That someone cared enough to send through God
Remembrance of my heavy burden and my special
   need of Him.
It was as if God's mercy
Transformed that prayer into an invisible see saw
Which lifted me while the weight of my burden
Rested briefly on the other end.
And with the lightened load, my tenseness thawed in
   the warm therapy of love and care
And new strength came now that I was more relaxed
   and trusting.
I knew that somewhere someone had prayed for me.[1]

Yes, intercessory prayer, the invisible see saw, made the difference. The new antiseptic world of the hospital didn't seem quite as formidable and impersonal. The unknown and as yet uncharted map of oncoming pain seemed somehow to be definable and bearable.

The preparations for my surgery moved with clocklike precision—blood pressuring, blood testing, blood "letting," punching, pricking, X-raying, and consulting. The fateful, slightly sedated ride "a la carte" from my room to surgery certainly would have done justice to a parading Caesar. After a final farewell glance at Carolyn, I was taken into the operating suite.

Here any personal bravado remaining in me was usurped. My next moments were lonely, suspended ones, devoid of reality and any semblance of being able to relate to a known quantity. It was an all unexplored green and white world in the operating arena. Alone. Stripped of status. Completely dependent. Not really expecting to return whole. Yet, an overarching prayer-engendered assurance permeated my consciousness—"God is with me. All those promises in the Word—they're true. You know there really isn't that great a terror in facing death. Please God, don't let that needle hurt me when I get this spinal block! Thank you. It didn't. Carolyn, I love you . . . Dear God, please be with . . ."

Eight hours later I was in the recovery room. From down the long corridor of subconsciousness I heard a voice echoing. It was my private-duty nurse, God's special minister in white, Kitty Small. "Wake up! Wake up," she said. "You're not in heaven. Kitty's here." Groggily I ventured one eye. It struggled to flutter open and then once again I collapsed into free-falling slumber.

Awareness arrived on waves of pain. A ripple of dull hurt began building on the distant horizon of somewhere. A single dissonance became a crescendo of thundering, oncoming cacophony. With ballooning, express-train speed, small swells built up into tidal waves of excruciating, all-engulfing pain. My frail craft of life was now to know the battering thrustings of suffering's unrelenting undertow.

During those next six weeks, I learned much about life and death as I made my down payment on Baptist Hospital.

For three weeks I had private duty, round-the-clock, special nurses. How tenderly they performed their tasks. But, oh how intense the pain and discomfort! Pain, I discovered, was not necessarily redemptive. Yet, if one can ride the crest of it until it crashes to its peak, pain can be a teacher.

It was the nighttime that seemed eternal. Even with Demerol-induced stupor, the grotesque shadows and strange nocturnal hospital sounds melted into episodes of fantasy. What strange dream sequences ebbed, flowed, and swirled around my wavering polarity of reality.

I edged toward death. How easy it would have been to slip on out. Yet, I fought for life. I held onto that tenuous thin line. I gained strange strength from hymns stored in my memory bank. I quoted them. I sang them. As the hospital bed seemed literally to fall and fall down some dark, never-ending, bottomless mine shaft, I sang! My parched lips had swollen and cracked. The nurses moistened them with tiny chips of ice.

The Levin tube, ever on guard, would unceremoniously pump back from my stomach each drop of melted ice or spoonful of proffered jello. "I am Thine, O Lord, I have heard Thy voice,/And it told Thy love to me;/But I long to rise in the arms of faith,/and be closer drawn to Thee." What a blessed assurance! I knew that underneath were the everlasting, supporting arms of God.

For eight weeks I recuperated at home. Then, gingerly at first, I resumed the teaching task at the seminary. The biggest surprise lay yet ahead. The inevitable series of postoperative tests and examinations were begun. The doctors once again punched and probed and X-rayed. Even though it was only January, I attempted to give up barium for Lent. The tests were completed. *There was no evidence of the malignancy to be found!* No trace of the cancerous growth was left. The team of specialists was mystified.

Something beyond the power of medical science had occurred!

As the recipient of this unexpected grace gift from God, I too, was amazed. Seventeen years later, I am still amazed. I cannot grasp fully the import of it all. Why should so many good people be taken by cancer and so few survive? Why suffering? Why should God seemingly supersede his own physical laws?

Quite frankly, I don't have these answers. I cannot fully explain what happened to me in that hospital room in New Orleans. I can only rest upon the knowledge that the prayers of myriads of agonizing, intercessory warriors bombarded God's throne of grace in my behalf. Prayer precipitated a twentieth-century miracle in my body. God in his mercy heard and answered—and healed!

Through these intervening years since my bout with cancer, I have forged out four immutable certainties. I have come to believe that these tested truths can sustain any Christian during times of crisis:

1. God is *able* in every trying circumstance of life.
2. God has the *right* to allow his children to be tested in the crucible of pain and trial.
3. God has an overriding *reason* for permitting us to suffer.
4. God has a *reward* through the suffering experience and in the aftermath of tribulation.

These four precepts have helped me catalog and put into true perspective not only my cancer experience, but also the petty, annoying day-by-day frustrations and failures that arise. I have come to the realization that I will, in all probability, be assailed frequently by unparalleled difficulties. But as his child, I can always count on him to deliver me. I have learned that whenever God puts a burden upon me, he will put his own arm underneath and sustain. Truly, "the Lord is my defense and my shield; my heart trusted in Him, and I am helped. Therefore my heart rejoices, and with my song I will praise him." (Ps. 28:7, Berkeley).

With My Song I Will Praise Him

"Don't Spare Me, Lord"

Forgive me Lord, I've prayed in vain that
You would spare me grief and pain.
But now my blinded eyes can see these things were
    best for me.
Don't spare me trouble if it will bring me close to
    Thee.
Don't spare me heartaches you bore a broken heart
    for me.
Don't spare me loneliness,
For I recall Gethsemane.
Don't spare me anything that you endured for me.

Don't spare me failure if this is what is best for me.
Don't spare me sickness if this will make me call on
    Thee.
Don't spare me suffering,
For I recall your agony.
Don't spare me anything that you endured for me.
But give me strength to follow Thee.[2]*

—Audrey Mieir

2 "Da Capo" Years

"Remember now thy Creator in the days of thy youth" (Eccl. 12:1).

Da capo is a wonderfully descriptive musical term. It literally means "go back to the beginning of the composition."

That is exactly what I did in the days and weeks of my convalescence. As the crashing confrontation of cancer's reality hit me and stunned shock slowly gave way to factual possibility of reoccurence, long-forgotten experiences began to emerge from the labyrinth of my mind.

Once before on a Boy Scout outing I had known such flashbacks. As a novice swimmer I ventured into water over my head. I started drowning—thrashing—going under for the third time! My twelve years of life rapidly and vividly pulsed on the picture-screen of memory. In a mere instant of time, past events paraded in review. Then—a rescuing hand of a buddy reached out and touched—and saved.

My cancer experience was similar to drowning. In the happening of my trauma I was thrashing about wildly, desperately for some meaning—any meaning for cancer. Faith undergoing testing ofttimes flays uncomprehendingly in the face of initial skirmishes with an unknown enemy. Because we're human, we can't easily and with immediacy convert and straighten out the question mark of "Why suffering?" into an affirmative exclamation point of "Praise!" That comes much later—only after agonizingly slow soul-searching.

In the aftermath of cancer surgery, one goes through times of readjustment. It is a wrenching happening to leave the womb of an encircling hospital and to enter once again the rough-and-tumble of a daily household routine. What if a need arises for a special-duty nurse—what if pain returns—what if sleep will not come at night—what if? After hospitalization it is quite common to go through valleys of doubt, perigees of despair, and hours of self-pity. A perfectly normal question faced time after time is, why me, Lord? or what have I done wrong to bring this affliction into my life? With suffering comes a swarm of Job-like questions that really have no discernible answers. Like those who have suffered since time immemorial, I too began that lonely venture of attempting to fit together the jagged, painful, jigsaw puzzle of what had happened to me—and why. Instinctively I turned the clock of time back and looked inward.

Carrollton Years

Childhood was spent in mid-America during those golden years following the end of the great depression. I was secure. Loved. An only child. With myriads of cousins and loving relatives, my early years were joyful, warm, and happy. Small-town America during the years preceding World War II approached a semblance of utopia. The pace was slow, persons knew persons, and material things didn't seem quite so important. Simplicity in needs prevailed. Wants seemed—at least in retrospect—within bounds. Recreation consisted of family croquet games, visiting out in the yard under starry skies, driving down to the Wabash to view the evening train go rushing from Kansas City to St. Louis or to see the Santa Fe Super-"Chief" literally fly by to Chicago. In October we attended Fall Festival on the town square, hunted chestnuts and roasted them, or hiked to Baby Canyon to shoot at squirrels (I never hit one). Winter brought out sleds and ice skates for frozen ponds—or nights spent by the fire playing Chinese Checkers, Monopoly, Old Maid, or writing jingles for soap contests. (I never won one!) Spring was utterly glorious in Missouri! What sheer luxury to feel the warmth of April's sun as it coaxed the flowers to bloom in extravagant array.

In January 1939, I felt strange stirrings. I became aware of my need for a personal Savior. How fortunate I was to be reared in a Christian home. Both my father and mother lived exemplary lives. It seemed so natural when they talked with me about letting Jesus come into my heart.

During a revival in my home church—First Baptist Church of Carrollton, Missouri—I accepted Christ as Savior. Dr. W. Frank Plainfield, an evangelist with the Home Mission Board, was the preacher. As the invitation was extended, I slipped out from the pew and walked to the front of the church. Dr. Merle Mitchell, our pastor, greeted me.

I felt a hand on my shoulder. It was my father. He joined me, making public his decision to become a Baptist. Our family was now one in Christ. We publicly affirmed this on February 11, 1939. My father and I were baptized side by side. The pilgrimage of following Christ had begun. A change had been wrought in my life. A process of *becoming* was underway.

On Sunday afternoon December 7, 1941, I was sitting

at our dining room table listening to the New York Phil-
harmonic weekly broadcast while painting in oils a pic-
ture-map of *Treasure Island*. The beauty of the orchestral
program was shattered by the detached, high-pitched, stac-
cato words of a news commentator who announced that
the Japanese had just bombed Pearl Harbor. An era of
American history closed that day and a new, terrifying,
bloody chapter of our national life began.

The war years brought changes to our high school.
Longtime friends left our town for service. Gold stars began
appearing in windows, giving mute testimony that a beloved son would never return home. Rationing of food
and gasoline began to pinch the good life we had known.
Interscholastic sports were suspended for the duration.
Albert Sutton, my classmate and fellow Eagle Scout, was
a war casualty. Life, I began to learn, had real sorrows.
People hurt. Friends disappointed. Yet God proved
overarching in his love. He led me on.

I was graduated in May 1945, and was selected to give
the salutatorian address. The speech was entitled "Freedom Under God." How bravely the words were spoken
to a crowded gymnasium—words which were delivered
from "head-memory" but certainly not "by heart." After
all, how can a seventeen-year-old possibly sense the full
impact and meaning of one's "freedom—under God"?

Army Years

In late May 1945, shortly after V-E Day, I was sworn
into the Army—a volunteer for the Army Specialized
Training Program. My years in service were rich, varied,
interesting, and certainly never dull. The first months were
spent in study at the University of Wyoming. When I

enlisted, I was promised Japanese Language School at Harvard University. Army reality militated. Instead of "ivy league" I was sent to engineering training at the University of Wyoming in Laramie. Basic training was in the great Northwest at Fort Lewis, Washington. Another six months was spent in the staging area of Fort Jackson, South Carolina. Finally, overseas assignment was made to Nüremberg, Germany. I was appointed Chaplain's Assistant in the 385th Station Hospital. Our hospital serviced the War Crimes Trial personnel. God was leading step-by-step according to his timing. He was preparing me for the future by allowing me to serve in a real-life, missionary situation.

My da capo years from 1947 onward can probably be best summed up in the following article which I wrote for the May 1950, issue of *The Baptist Student.*

"Graduation at Mid-Century"
Graduation! This is it. Yesterday's tomorrow has arrived. Futuristic freshman dreams have suddenly been transformed from a day in the dim beyond into the actuality of now—a buzzing crowd of proud parents and loved ones . . . the rustle of academic gowns . . . breeze-excited tassels . . . "Pomp and Circumstance" music . . . sheepskins . . . "Auld Lang Syne." Can this be real?

It seems such a short time since that spring morning when time stopped in its flight and those three most familiar commands, "Name! Rank! Serial Number!" ushered into existence the higher education of 17187922.

It was all strangely different from idealistically enshrined dreams of ivy tower learning. Soon, however, our allotted six months of study were over. In the twenty months following this brief sojourn in college, events that educate one in the great university of life passed in rapid succession—basic training which meant marching in full field pack under a blazing sun; replacement depots with their endless rounds of roll calls, inoculations, rumors, and shakedown inspections; a close-packed cruise over the bounding main in a troopship; work as a chaplain's assistant in a station hospital in the war ravaged American Zone of occupied Germany; visiting and amateurishly shutterbugging for posterity some of those faraway places with strange sounding names; organizing youth rallies and Sunday Schools for both American and German young people; experiencing the joy of seeing a former Hitler youth won to Christ; redeployment; discharge; home.

School began again in September 1947. With it came my decision and conviction that a college education was a supremely important must, that there was a need to gain more knowledge of the past and of the present in order to face the future more intelligently. My life has been profoundly influenced, changed, and channeled as a result of that decision.

Today the time has come to leave behind the old hill and her halls of learning. With this parting comes the necessity to face up honestly to the question, What does college *really* mean to me? Here is what I find.

My college means the best years of my life, years made up of hundreds of precious little experiences—freshman caps, bonfires, jalopies, seining muddy ponds for biology specimens, Russian I, youth revivals, term papers, opera rehearsals, B.S.U. council meetings, homecoming parades, library fines, glee club, sleepily plodding to 7:50 classes, keeping a scrapbook of clippings, Achievement Day—when outstanding alumni came back to the campus to give their philosophy for success in their chosen fields, prayer-mates, sharing a sunset, cramming for final exams, bull sessions in the wee small hours, Student Night at Christmas, morning watch, answered prayers, summer mission service.

My college life has meant a closer and more personal walk with Christ. It has meant Religious Focus Weeks with their down-to-earth formulas for attaining the higher happiness through consecration of all to him. It was in a Religious Focus Week that I made my full surrender to and acceptance of *his* blueprint for my life.

For over a year I doggedly pursued a premed course when I knew in my heart of hearts that it wasn't his will for me. I rationalized and said, "Lord, I'll be a medical missionary, if you will just let me be a doctor."

But he had other plans. There in the high spiritual moment of that morning chapel service he spoke to me. Every word from the speaker's lips was custom-tailored, it seemed, to fit my stubbornness. I argued, "Of course, I love to sing, Lord. You have blessed me with a voice. It is fine to have music as a hobby, but not for my life's work!"

The speaker said "A man's gift maketh room for him, and bringeth him before great men" (Prov. 18:16). Use the gift that the Lord had given you. The gleaming white love shafts of God's truth pierced my heart. In that moment of surrender to his will, the clouds of darkness that had veiled my life from his smile were dispersed.

The heavenly sunshine that rushed into my soul outshone that which streamed into the chapel through the golden stained-glass windows. I can personally testify that if we just let go and let God have his wonderful way in our lives, he will open "the windows of heaven, and pour . . . out a blessing" (Mal. 3:10).

Lastly, my college has given me the assurance that I am more fully prepared to face the problems and question marks of the future. We who are graduates at this pivotal point in the twentieth century have as our main responsibility the winning of the world to Christ Jesus.

Let us be convinced without a doubt that Christ is the *only* answer for these troubled times. Let us catch the vision of Christ-centered service in every realm of our lives. Let us attempt great things for God and expect great things from God.

May our prayer ever be "Oh, God, help us to accept the fact that life is not what we know and plan it to be, but what we trust in and dare to do for Thee!"

Let us go forth then, confident that he holds our future in his hands.

With My Song I Will Praise Him

"Precious Lord, Take My Hand"

Precious Lord, take my hand,
Lead me on, help me stand;
I am tired, I am weak, I am worn;
Thru the storm, thru the night,
Lead me on to the light;
Take my hand, precious Lord, lead me home.[1]*

*By Thomas Dorsey. Copyright 1938 by Chappell Music Co. Used by permission.

3 A Man's Gift Makes Room for Him

"A man's gift makes room for him" (Prov. 18:16, RSV).

Beginnings

It is truly amazing how God sends the *right* people into our lives at the exact time we have a need. Fred Smith was God's living message to me during Religious Focus Week, 1948, at William Jewell College. As a sophomore I was pursuing a premed course—not because of a burning conviction that God was leading but because it was more or less expected that I follow in the footsteps of my brilliant cousin who was an outstanding vascular surgeon. Like many post-World War II college students, I was drifting— no real goal to galvanize, marshal, and possess.

Then on a winter morning in chapel, Fred Smith spoke. He came on like the proverbial gang buster! After almost three decades I can still hear him say, "I'll give any one in this audience this crisp new $20.00 bill if they can quote for me Proverbs 18:16." Many of us reached for our pocket New Testaments and then sheepishly remembered that Proverbs is in the Old Testament. Fred Smith used this technique to burn into our minds the text of Proverbs 18:16. "A man's gift makes room for him and brings him before great men," quoted Fred Smith. "Or translated into twentieth-century lingo," he said, "Use the gift that God has given *you,* and he will bless you, and you will stand before great men as equals and there witness to them of God's goodness to you!''

Those words made sense to me. In honesty I was seeking to know what God would have me do with my life. I certainly wasn't happy in premed. He had given me a gift in music, but I somehow was holding back and not giving him free rein in this area of my life. I personally did not want to pursue music vocationally. I suppose I felt musicians were a peculiar lot, relegated to living in a garret somewhere, following a bohemian life-style, eating French bread, growing long hair, and developing dandruff. No, I did not especially want to become a professional musician. But Fred Smith's words kept haunting me: "Use the gift that God has given you, and he will bless you. God will use *you!*" Like a constant timpani roll, the words of Proverbs 18:16 pulsed through my mind and being. *"Use* your gift! Use *your* gift! Use your *gift!"* In all candor I had to admit God had endowed me with a talent. I had discovered while in the army that he had given me the ability to communicate through singing. It was strange. I could stand before a group and sing and share his love and goodness. People listened and were seemingly moved. It was something beyond my ability—it was God's grace gift to me. It had to be used! And so, calmly, rationally, and in a conscious act of my will, I prayed in chapel that morning that God would take my gift and use it. I gave back to him my music. Nothing complicated. Nothing really that complex or profound. A simple act of faith and will. No sirens! No bells! No smoking, burning bushes! And yet a sense of awe overtook me. A change took place, for now I belonged to him. He was not only my Savior; he was also my *Lord.*

A new facet of meaning came into my life as I realized

that God would have me take honest stock of myself to find out what gift he had given me. I was free to discover—to develop—and most important of all, to give my gift back to him.

Through Days of Preparation

Within a few weeks after my commitment of my song to him, I was invited to be guest soloist at the Southern Baptist Convention in Oklahoma City. About a month later, I was selected as one of the fourteen Baptist Student Union Summer Missionaries to be sent to the Hawaiian Islands by fellow students from throughout the South. How amazing that a Missouri lad with a rural background and a mere modicum of a gift would serve as a missionary in Hawaii. And beyond that—still another blessing. It was during those 1949 summer days that I met and served with Carolyn Turnage, Florida's student missionary. The islands worked their magic. Two years later Carolyn was to become my bride.

When I returned from Hawaii for my senior year at William Jewell College, a very full schedule of speaking and singing opportunities throughout the entire Southern Baptist Convention opened for me. I was graduated in May 1950, and entered Missouri University for master's work in European history. My chosen research project was centered in the personal library of Charles Haddon Spurgeon. This repository was housed at William Jewell College. During this year of graduate work in history and researching the great Baptist leader's contributions at Metropolitan Tabernacle, I learned the discipline of waiting on the Lord for the next step. It came.

In March 1951, I was invited by Dr. Harold G. Sanders

to lead the music in a revival at First Baptist Church of Tallahassee, Florida. After that meeting I was extended a call by the church to become their minister of music. On September 1, 1951, my new bride of five days and I began our ministry in this strategic church. Serving there afforded me the chance to work on my second bachelor's degree—this time in music—and a master's degree in music education at Florida State University.

New Orleans Baptist Theological Seminary
1954—1963

In the summer of 1954, the late Dr. Roland Q. Leavell, then president of New Orleans Baptist Theological Seminary, asked me to join the faculty of the school of church music at his institution. Dr. Plunkett Martin, beloved dean of the school of church music, had faith in me and had made the recommendation. Carolyn and I moved to New Orleans in August 1954, where I began my work at the seminary and as minister of music at historic Saint Charles Avenue Baptist Church.

Our decade in New Orleans was an extremely happy one. New and varied facets of ministry developed—my first LP record album, *Claude Rhea Sings,* produced in 1955 by Word Records, revival engagements, appearances with symphony orchestras and in oratorios, and the new role of father. Babies, I soon found, were not as fragile as they at first seem to be.

In the summer of 1955, I went to Columbia University in New York City to do advanced work in educational administration. While in New York, I served as tenor soloist at Calvary Baptist Church. A worldwide ministry through shortwave radio broadcasts was afforded me as soloist in that famous metropolitan church.

The summer of 1957 found my family and me back at Florida State University in Tallahassee. My goal—to complete my doctorate. A second LP album was released that year with Clifford Tucker and the Calvary Baptist Church Radio Choir. My friend and fellow choir member, Van Cliburn, lustily sang (not played) in the vocal ensemble.

The long-sought doctor's degree was awarded me by Florida State University in August 1958. With high hopes, the Rhea family returned to the seminary in New Orleans to resume my teaching career. Two months later during a routine physical checkup my physician discovered I had cancer. For almost three months, routine living ground to a halt while I fought for my life.

By January of 1959, I was able to resume my teaching responsibilities. Opportunity came to cut another album. *Blessed Assurance* was recorded in Chicago in the midst of a paralyzing blizzard. Still weak from my surgery, I was forced to stretch out on the studio floor and rest between recording "takes."

In June of 1959, Carolyn and I flew to Rüschlikon, Switzerland, where I was guest lecturer at the first European Baptist Church Music Conference. This significant meeting was held at the International Baptist Theological Seminary. While in Europe, I recorded *Majestic Themes* with the London Symphony Orchestra.

The following summer, I was invited back to the seminary in Rüschlikon to lecture for the six-week summer session. At that time I worked with leaders from eleven different Baptist constituencies in Europe. I presented my first series of sacred concerts for the Foreign Mission Board in Spain and Denmark.

The summer of 1960 was a rare point in time to take

the pulsebeat of Baptist life in Spain, for evangelicals were still being "persecuted for righteousness sake." Missionary Joe Mefford and I traveled through the provinces of Spain and sang and preached the gospel.

It was while lecturing in Rüschlikon that I received a cable from President Leo Eddleman stating that I had been named dean of the School of Church Music at New Orleans Baptist Theological Seminary. Now it seemed that permanent roots were to be put down in New Orleans, and I would spend the rest of my life teaching and administering a seminary music school.

Mission opportunities still came, however. In the summer of 1961, I was invited by the Home Mission Board to work in revivals and to give sacred concerts in Panama. While there I served with both the Panamanians and with the Cuna Indians of the San Blas Islands. I discovered that music related and can carry the message of Christ, even in very primitive cultures.

The Foreign Mission Board contacted me in 1962 about the possibilities of carrying out musical pilot projects in several countries around the world. I accepted the challenge and in late winter of 1963 went to the Middle East, presenting concerts in Lebanon, Jordan, and Israel. From the Middle East I traveled to Indonesia. For two weeks, Dr. Lewis Smith, my medical missionary/accompanist, and I gave concerts throughout that emerging nation. From Indonesia we journeyed to the Federation of Malaysia and there under the sponsorship of Malaysian Baptists presented "standing room only" concerts in Victoria Hall in Singapore. Enroute to Japan, our final destination, concerts were sung in the Crown Colony of Hong Kong. There, in City Hall Auditorium, a very influential segment of the Chinese community was reached through the medium of sacred concerts.

My 1963 pioneering tour ended in Japan, where I participated in the major rallies of the Japan New Life Movement. As soloist with the very excellent Nippon Symphony Orchestra, I visited many of the large population centers of Japan. A highlight of the entire tour was singing "Blessed Redeemer" (in Japanese) just before Dr. Baker James Cauthen preached. It was a humbling experience to communicate with some forty thousand Japanese people in their own tongue. The spirit of God moved that night in the stadium in Tokyo. Hundreds of people came forward to profess faith in Christ as Savior.

Houston Baptist College
1963—1967

During the early spring days of 1963 I was faced with a perplexing decision. God seemed to be leading from the seminary to service at the newly founded Houston Baptist College in Houston, Texas. Convinced of the rightness of the timing and the evolving dimensions of opportunity, I accepted the invitation of President W. H. Hinton to become chairman of the Division of Fine Arts at the new college.

It was quite a change of pace to adjust from comfortable, secure, seminary life to a booming, aborning college. In seminary the young people had already discovered a definite direction and course for their life. In college most of the students were still seeking to find their way and to discover their personhood. Curriculum for a new school had to be devised. The challenging problems of beginnings had to be faced. Out of nothing, a new institution was formed.

The experience of learning to communicate with the

"restless ones" of the college generation of the 1960s was no mean feat. I had to stretch painfully and grow. My concepts of personal self-worth, stewardship of life and Christian world view underwent reexamination and evaluation. God showed me˙ that as his disciple I could not remain static or unblinkingly secure during times of world upheaval. I must be viable in my career development. I must be ever open and accepting in my appropriation of his grace gifts.

Claiming Proverbs 18:16 had now led to another exciting chapter of the pilgrimage. I was named administrative vice-president of Houston Baptist College in 1965. Newer and richer and fuller outlets for service appeared. I glimpsed fresh, untried vistas. Facets of administrative experience in public relations, financial planning, student enlistment, alumni affairs, and student personal challenges were mine. Houston, a rapidly expanding megalopolis deep in the heart of Texas, was the crucible for a unique, noble experiment in Christian higher education. By using my gift, I found blessings beyond measure. My career in education was pointing more and more toward top administration.

Foreign Mission Board
1967—1969

At first it was like a gentle Gulf breeze. The warm, persuasive, ever-convicting hint of God's finger pointing and his hand providing. The tenuous, subtle nudge became firm, entrenched conviction. "A man's gift makes room for him." The subsequent course of events and happenings naturally confluenced into world missions. Loose threads seemingly disjunct and disarrayed began to fall into place. It *is* true what Dr. Chester Swor once said at Ridgecrest

Assembly: "There is never any waste in the will of God."
In God's divine economy, every scrap, each event is woven
into the tapestry of one's life story. God was leading me
unmistakably toward service with the Baptist Foreign Mission Board.

Our eldest son, C³, was not at all certain we should
abandon the vibrant Texas happening at Houston Baptist
College for the unknown of the Foreign Mission Board.
He had deep feelings in the matter. One evening, he scrib-
bled a note to me in his sixth-grade hieroglyphics.

> Dear Daddy,
>   I'm not for the move to Virginia. It's not fair. I
> love our home here in Houston and the yard which
> Grandma and I spent so much time on. Besides that,
> I have lots of friends at school and at church and
> in Boy Scouts. Please don't leave the college.
>   I hope this letter doesn't hurt you, but I vote *against*
> moving to Richmond. Love,
>
>   Your son,
>   C³

I hadn't expected that degree of foot-dragging on the
home front. I pondered several days before answering my
son's letter. I prayed and searched for a dimension of
wisdom beyond my grasp.

Mr. Claude Rhea, III
7711 Beechnut
Houston, Texas 77036

Dear C³,

    I have read and reread your letter to me written
on April 11, 1967. Each time I read it I see my son,

my firstborn child, in a wonderful new light. You are growing into young manhood, son, and are beginning to feel some of the pressures and disappointments of real life. You see, as one grows into adulthood, he must begin to accept life as it realistically is, not as he ideally would have it to be.

Yes, son, I am hurt by your letter—hurt in a way that only a dad can feel. The hurt is a mixed-up one. I'm sad because this honest expression of your feelings about our moving to Richmond, Virginia, reflects the fact that you're no longer a child—you're even now sensing the inborn stirrings to become an adult and begin life on your own. This is a hurt which every parent must face. It's a part of life itself.

Secondly, I'm sad because my decision has caused you pain. Son, I wish I could bear this for you, but I can't. I realize it is going to be difficult to leave our lovely home, and Grandma's flowers, your school, your friends, and your Scout troop. But C³, security is not a house or yard or even friends. Security is Mother and Daddy's love for *you* and God's love for us all. Our love for you has not changed—if anything it has grown even deeper. Richmond, Virginia, will offer many fresh opportunities to have new experiences and friends. Indeed, you will have the chance to mature and to build upon what God has already given you.

Daddy knows that God has called him to this new ministry with the Foreign Mission Board. How I pray that you too will know and feel that God is leading our family to this new place of service. In all the 12 wonderful years you have been my son, I've never been more proud of you than today. You trusted your

father enough to tell him exactly how you feel about
a matter. I appreciate your honesty! Real men are
always honest. I love you, son.

Devotedly yours,

Dad

My letter to C³ was the means for helping me crystalize
and make final my rationale for joining the staff of the
Foreign Mission Board. C³ matured through this decision.
So did I. He cast his ballot to move to Richmond. That
made it unanimous.

My two- and one-half year sojourn as consultant in music
and mass communications for the Board was the most
personally fulfilling chapter of my entire life. I sang, traveled, conceptualized ideas, served, and expanded the
boundaries of my world view to undreamed-of proportions.
The world was my "beat." Working closely with Dr. Joseph
Underwood, consultant in evangelism and church development and with Dr. Winston Crawley, director of the
Overseas Division of the Foreign Mission Board, I planned
music strategy for crusades in many countries. Operational
procedures with music missionaries were devised, struc-
tured, and adapted for differing cultures. Conferences were
held on mission fields. Music was studied and explored
as a tool of proclamation—as a vehicle for telling the old,
old story in a fresh and new way.

As the role of consultant in music evolved, the joy of
unlimited opportunity for planning, proclaiming, and
working with missionaries on the fields and with spiritual
giants on the Richmond staff was tempered with the realization that one lifetime would not be enough. "A man's
gift makes room for him." True. But limitations of strength

and factors of the human equation circumscribe each one of us. The totality of the world missions task is an overwhelming one. It is impossible when viewed in strictly human terms. The enormity of human suffering, hurt, need, and lostness can crush and frustrate. What can one person, one mere life, one set of gifts possibly achieve? How can even a small dent be made in the engulfing needs of lost mankind?

While doing research for Lottie Moon Week of Prayer programs in *Royal Service,* Carolyn found a quote from Colin Morris which spoke directly to my dilemma: "The most the average Christian can hope to do is to take hold of the *near edge* of a great problem and act at some cost to himself."

This was a partial answer at least. I could only address myself to "near edges" of great problems and act upon them. I learned that even as a world missionary I was not expected to bear the burden of the whole world alone. I had to put into perspective that it is the work God does *through* us that counts, not what we do for him. Oswald Chambers in his book *My Utmost for His Highest* helped me come to terms with this fact:

The snare in Christian work is to rejoice in successful service, to rejoice in the fact that God has used you. You never can measure what God will do through you if you are rightly related to Jesus Christ. Keep your relationship right with Him, then whatever circumstances you are in, and whoever you meet day by day, He is pouring rivers of living water through you, and it is of His mercy that He does not let you know it . . . remember that wherever you are, you are put there by God; and by the reaction of your life on the circumstances around you, you will fulfill

God's purpose, as long as you keep in the light as God is in the light.[1]

The pressures and self-imposed rigors of being out of the country for over 70 percent of the time began to take their toll. Our middle son Randy was bruised by my extended absences. At first, I would not concede that anyone in Christian work could have this type of problem. I was, after all, called to a specific task. I was honestly seeking first to serve God . . . to use my gifts. Randy rebelled. In the home. At school. At church. He was impelled and disturbed by forces which he could neither understand nor quell. The "near edge" of a great need had to be addressed—not only in Bangkok but in our home in Richmond, Virginia. The cry to help was undeniable.

I attempted to express these growing convictions in my final report to the Foreign Mission Board in session in Dallas, Texas, on May 7, 1969.

A New Dimension in Discipleship

Today I've asked for a point of personal privilege—the privilege of speaking from my heart to yours—to share with you a growing conviction that has become mine—a revelation and concomitant acceptance of a new dimension in discipleship.

My pilgrimage like yours has been characterized by God's encompassing goodness and unbounding grace—through many dangers (I reflect even now upon the fact of God's intervention in sparing me from cancer), toils and strife, I have already come—but God's wondrous grace has led me safe thus far and certainly will lead me on.

The events pointing toward my life commitment with the Foreign Mission Board have been unique—childhood interest in missions, army service attached to War Crimes Trials in Nüremberg, B.S.U. summer missionary to Hawaii, minister of music, soloist, the ministry of a recording artist, seminary professor and dean of the School of Church Music at New Orleans Baptist Theological Seminary, dean of Fine Arts and then administrative vice-president of Houston Baptist College, and a wonderful, wholesome, understanding family that backed me in a decision to come to Richmond to serve as the Board's first consultant in Music and Mass Communications.

I can never begin to express adequately the joy, the holy privilege that has been mine these two and one-half years: (1) traveling up and down the world witnessing through song, (2) sharing Christ through concerts, radio-TV in forty-one countries, (3) "spreading abroad the fragrance of the knowledge of the love of God." Such joy is unspeakable.

Upon this scene has come a cloud, however—a cloud no larger than a man's hand—in reality a cloud no larger than the hand of a lad of twelve, my son—my son Randy. How to verbalize this tenderness is difficult. It is the persistent, unrelenting, demanding, baseball-sweaty, disturbed hand of a boy who needs his father and needs him *now* in an in-depth relationship over the period of the next few years.

Herein is the trauma of decision that has been mine—herein is the loneliness of reevaluation and determination of God's will for me.

My decision has been wrought out through long hours of international airplane rides, in hotel rooms in faraway places with strange sounding names—a

decision which has led to a new dimension in personal discipleship, a realization that
   —along with one's stewardship of God-given talents channeled to a lost world
   —must be a balanced portfolio of investment of one's self in his God-given family.

This morning I feel constrained to share with you my friends and colleagues a new facet in my pilgrimage—to invite you to "share my heart" before the official press release of my decision. The God of grace and God of glory has led me to a new mission field—a university campus! There, hopefully, some father-son relationships can be cemented simultaneously with strategic administrative leadership responsibilities which I've been asked to assume.

Samford University in Birmingham will be my new mission field beginning September 1, 1969. I have asked Dr. Cauthen to accept my resignation effective that date. I covet your prayers my dear friends for
   —Christ-likeness in acceptance of an inevitable fact
   —growth in understanding and patience
   —wisdom and courage for the facing of this particular hour.

I covet your prayers for a fresh understanding of how to go into my God-appointed world of the university and share the gospel.

I go with joy because the Lord is my only strength.

Resolution

WHEREAS: It is said that God counts not time by years, so it is that the ministry of Claude H. Rhea, Jr. cannot possibly be mea-

sured by the two- and one-half years he
served the Lord through the Foreign
Mission Board; and

WHEREAS: It is true also that there are no vital
statistics by which one can measure the
success of this Music and Communications ministry; and

WHEREAS: Perhaps it could be learned how many
songs he sang in concerts in more than
forty countries, but how does one measure the spiritual impact of such programs? and

WHEREAS: No one can determine the influence of
that one life for two- and one-half years
in its contact with hundreds of missionaries; now therefore

BE IT RESOLVED:

THAT, we, the members of the Foreign
Mission Board of the Southern Baptist
Convention, shall try in these few words
to thank Claude for his unselfish and
devoted service; and

THAT we commend him to the administration and Faculty of Samford University, and

THAT it is our conviction that Claude
Rhea is God's servant who will wherever he serves, represent Jesus Christ in
a worldwide ministry marked by his
gracious spirit and his magnificent musical talent; and

THAT we highly resolve, as co-laborers
with Claude Rhea, to express to him
our love and gratitude, to assure him

of our prayers and our moral support
as he takes up his work at Samford
University; and
THAT we pledge to him our undying
friendship in the gospel of the One
whose we are and whom we represent.
By action of the Foreign Mission Board in Glorieta,
New Mexico, in business session, August 20, 1969.

Samford University
1969—Present

These seven years at Samford have been delightful ones.
Birmingham is a special place. How my cup of contentment
brims to overflowing! Our School of Music has been
blessed and blessed again. Present here are those magic
ingredients of talented, wonderful students, dedicated,
well-trained faculty, and well-appointed and equipped
facilities.

Since 1969 our school of music has more than tripled
in size, moving from 80 students to over 250. A "common-
wealth of the arts" is flourishing here. A new eight million
dollar Fine Arts Center provides the latest in technical
"hardware" for training young people in the age-old art
of music. The pendulum has swung full-sweep. As dean,
I stand in a leadership role, given the freedom to "dream
the impossible dream" and attempt to put feet under the
achievement of things thought unattainable. As new classes
of eager freshmen fill the ranks year by year, I sense fresh
challenges to pass on to yet another generation age-old
truths: God knows your name! He is interested in your
life and your contribution to history.

I have found it increasingly true—"a man's gift makes

room for him." Since that day in long ago 1948, the abiding promise of Proverbs 18:16 has been a keystone in my philosophy of vocation. Time after time the words of this proverb have rung true. God honors and keeps his promises—even in the twentieth century. He is interested in each one of us personally and in our *becoming*. That unbelievable chain of events which began to unfold after I said, and meant it, "God, I am willing to be used of you; I truly want to use the gift that you have given me," continues its ongoing surge. The excitement of letting God channel his love through you is matchless. Sometimes, in retrospect, I stand in genuine awe. For even as I have catalogued on these pages the scope of God's blessings on me, "I scarce can take it in."

In steady, patient, unmistakable ways, God has continually led. His timetable has been correct. The structuring of vocational parameters certain. This one thing I know— "A man's gift makes room for him."

With My Song I Will Praise Him

"Day by Day"

Day by day and with each passing moment,
    Strength I find to meet my trials here;
Trusting in my Father's wise bestowment,
    I've no cause for worry or for fear.
He whose heart is kind beyond all measure
    Gives unto each day what he deems best—
Lovingly, its part of pain and pleasure,
    Mingling toil with peace and rest.

                    —CAROLINE V. SANDELL-BERG

4 Because

"For this cause shall a man leave father and mother, and shall cleave to his wife" (Matt. 19:5).

For a number of years I used as an encore number at my concerts a traditional Appalachian ballad entitled "Sporting Bachelors." It began with these words:

Come all you sporting bachelors
who wish to get good wives.
Oh don't be deceived as I am.
I married me a wife, makes me
weary of my life,
She makes me strive and do all that I can,
She makes me strive and do all that I can.

As a bachelor I sang this jingle many times. I supposed the words must be true. After all, audiences laughed heartily each time I performed it.

Then in the summer of 1949, I met a young lady who changed my words and tune completely. Carolyn Turnage was Florida's summer missionary to Hawaii. I was Missouri's representative. We met in Los Angeles before the flight to the Rainbow Islands. Our acquaintance was polished during the week of missionary orientation. An indepth friendship was quickened and blossomed into love as we daily worked together at University Baptist Church in Honolulu. Our first outing was lunch under the famous banyan tree at the Moana Hotel. The broadcast *Hawaii Calls* was in progress. Traditional island melodies were being beamed to the Mainland. The waves crashed into Waikiki. Trade winds rustled palm fronds. The overpowering scent of plumeria and yellow ginger blossoms perfumed the air. Diamond Head wavered in and out of focus through the glare of sunlight on the beach. Now you must admit that was *quite* a setting for our first date!

Those six weeks of missionary service brought Carolyn and me to the realization that we had much in common yet much in diversity. We began to sense areas of our own incompleteness which found complement only in the other person. A summer short-subject romance had all the potentialities of becoming a main attraction.

We flew back to the Mainland in August. Carolyn returned to Florida and I to Missouri. We wondered if Ma Bell's telephone conversations and Uncle Sam's mail service could suffice to nurture our deepening love for each other.

Christmas, 1949, I migrated southward for the holidays. My first contact with true Southern living was in the sleepy little North Florida town of Chattahoochee. I had my first introduction to grits, wild turkey, dressing "sack," sweet potato soufflé, and black-eyed peas.

Carolyn was even more wonderful than I remembered. Many a dream for future days was shared as we sat on the sofa and watched the crackling, pungent logs flickering in the fireplace.

The new decade of the 1950s was ushered in at a church watch night service. I returned to Missouri and my final semester at William Jewell College.

It seemed that June would never come that year. I rode

the train to Florida for Carolyn's graduation from Florida State University. I couldn't afford to fly. The diamond engagement ring had absorbed all my assets plus any anticipated cash flow. On a campus bench under a wide spreading pecan tree, I asked Carolyn to become my life partner. She said, YES!

As I slipped the engagement ring onto her finger, I said, "This ring, dear, is symbolic of our life together: JOY, SORROW, SERVICE. I paid for part of the ring with money earned singing at weddings. That's JOY! Some with money from being paid soloist at a funeral home. That's SORROW! Most of it, however, came from my salary as minister of music. And that's *SERVICE!*"

We celebrated our silver anniversary on August 26, 1976. As we reviewed and took stock of our marriage relationship at this strategic benchmark, Carolyn and I both agreed that these twenty-five years have indeed been good ones. Those three words spoken the night of our formal engagement were to some extent prophetic. Our marriage has been characterized by much joy, some sorrow, and ample service opportunities.

Joy

At times in our marriage we have been utterly surprised by joy. The night before our wedding, friends in Chattahoochee hosted an outdoor reception for us. Food and punch were served in a formal garden. Bowers of fragrant, blooming flowers served as living decorations. As scores of friends greeted us, an old farm wagon decked out with roses and greenery was slowly pulled into the yard by an indolent old South Georgia mule. Flowers bedecked his harness. A male quartet serenaded us from the wagon bed:

"I love you truly, truly dear. Life with its sorrow, life with
its tears. Fade into dreams when I feel you are near. For
you love me truly, truly dear."

Our wedding day was celebrated with paeans of music,
two ministers, and an air conditioner that malfunctioned.
It was so hot in the sanctuary that the candles melted into
inverted horseshoes. Just as my bride, a vision of loveliness
in billowy white lace, approached the altar with her father,
I stepped forward and sang to her. "Because you come
to me with nought save love." Only the conditioned response of singing a solo kept me from quaking.

Highlights of joy have been ours through these years—the
joys of parenting three totally individual children; decorat-
ing our home in our own style; round the world travel;
rare, quiet evenings spent in reading; composing and writing two children's music books as a team; completing my
doctorate and after graduation placing the doctoral hood
on Carolyn; conducting prayer seminars together; learning
new skills to share; knowing you're loved and accepted
as you are. Yes, marriage has brought joy beyond measure.

Lord, I thank you for "this vast treasure of content that
is mine today." Amen.

Sorrow

Our marriage has also been tempered by totally unexpected adversity. How shocked we were to learn that the
world didn't stop after our first marital quarrel. We've
discovered that humor can help dilute angry feelings. Soon
after we were married, I purchased symbolic gifts for our
home—the "harmony pot" and the "trouble book." Whenever we argued about something and disharmony reigned,
I, as head of the household, would ceremoniously lift out
the "harmony pot" (a small flower pot) from its burnished

copper, musical staff mounting on the wall and then proceed to make an official entry in our family "trouble book." I always would present the document for Carolyn to cosign. After reading the generally hilarious distortion of our disagreement, we were able to laugh about it; and harmony was restored.

As we have moved onward into marriage, as mutual ties have strengthened and our thought processes have melded, Carolyn and I have been strangely supported in our mutual dependence upon each other and upon God. Time after time we have cast ourselves completely on his unfailing, undying love. Sometimes as the deep waters of sorrow have swept over us, we have wondered if the struggle is bearable—the death of Carolyn's parents, financial reverses, sick children, personal bouts with cancer, extended hospitalization, a runaway son. Yet, in spite of all these pressures (and many more) our marriage has survived. It has floated, not floundered, in the face of storms.

Thank you, Lord, that even while we were going through great trials you have "given a song in the night season and all the day long." Amen.

Service

One of life's greatest adventures is to ascertain God's leadership and to discover his will as he unfolds, day by day, opportunities for service. As our marriage has matured, Carolyn and I have been amazed at the fresh discipleship outlets afforded us. We have slowly come to the conclusion that the *where* and *what* of vocation are not of optimum importance. It is our availability to him that really counts.

Each vocational opportunity appropriated has had its own peculiar set of blessings and reward. We have long since learned that "every work for Jesus will be blessed"—maybe not in the exact way we planned, but blessed nonetheless. For within the economy of his divine timetable, work for the Master is miraculously multiplied like the loaves and fishes. In spite of our puny humanity, God will channel his love to others through us.

For the most part, Carolyn and I have enjoyed our diverse avenues for service. In fact, we've had fun. As husband and wife, our individual and collective ministries have embraced teaching on the high school, college, university, and seminary levels; world mission service; administrative responsibilities; writing devotional books, a cookbook, numerous articles; composing children's music collections; mass media involvements; concert tours; recording LP albums; conducting prayer seminars; extensive world travel. There is all this and more—so much more yet to anticipate.

Service for God yields blessings, and blessings when counted, give rise to gratitude. Personal gratitude and thanksgiving must be translated into "thanks-living." In turn, the theme of the thankfully lived life is love. It is by love that we are compelled to serve him.

Lord, I'm grateful that you put your disciples where they will glorify you, and that they are not judges at all of where that is or should be. Amen.

And now there abides in our marriage, joy, sorrow, and service. These three. Attributes which give meaning and substance to life itself.

With My Song I Will Praise Him

"O Perfect Love"

O perfect Love, all human thought transcending,

Lowly we kneel in prayer before Thy throne,
That theirs may be the love which knows no ending,
Whom Thou forevermore dost join in one.

O perfect Life, be Thou their full assurance
Of tender charity and steadfast faith,
Of patient hope and quiet, brave endurance,
With child-like trust that fears no pain nor death.

Grant them the joy which brightens earthly sorrow;
Grant them the peace which calms all earthly strife,
And to life's day the glorious unknown morrow
That dawns upon eternal love and life.

                              —DOROTHY R. GURNEY

5 Sing While You Grow

"I will sing with the understanding also" (1 Cor. 14:15).

Parenting is a puzzling, disjunct-conjunct happening. The pendulum of child-parent relationships is constantly, predictably, measuredly swinging—yet is simultaneously ever-changing in its kaleidoscopic irregularity. Where else in the world is there such a viable, shifting scene as that existing within the child-rearing experience? Where else within the confines of short segments of time can one pulse from festival to funeral, from lofty idealism to fundamental realism, from refreshing joy to dry desert?

If I have learned one clarion, eternal lesson from dealing with our children, it is this—man that is born of woman has it uphill all the way in this life! Life is a struggle. One doesn't climb over obstacles by elevator or escalator but rather by struggling round by round up and over his particular chain of mountains. "Child raisin' " isn't an easy hill in our pilgrimage. On the contrary, it's a steep crag beset with pitfalls and crevasses. Yet in those rare, supreme moments when the full impact of being a purveyor of part of the sacred tissue of humanity is personally comprehended, a sense of awe overtakes us. Carl Sandburg once wrote, "A baby is God's opinion that the world should go on." As parents we're a part of the ongoingness of the human race. By conscious will we can choose to bring

children into the world. We're richer and wiser because
of our children.

How shortchanged Carolyn and I would have been without a baby's diapers to change, 2:00 A.M. bottles to feed,
earaches, chicken pox, measles, mumps, bumped heads
and scraped knees to nurse, burped-on blue serge suits
to sponge, childish laughter to hear, and slobbery kisses
to receive.

Several years ago my wife penned the following words
in her book *Such Is My Confidence:*

"Home"

The family is the divine pattern of existence. Each
family grows from the same pattern, yet each can
be quite different.

The quality of material, the choice of color; imagina-
tive design, care given details—even trim and acces-
sories—all have a part of the finished effect.

Thus, the home becomes either a duplicate of mass
production or a fresh and exciting creation.[1]

We have attempted through the years to use music as
a means of making our home a fresh and exciting creation.
We have found that children and music are inseparably
linked. It seems that almost any facet of a child's life can
be expressed in song.

In casting about as a family for realistic life situations
to sing about and to help teach God's great, unchanging
truths to our children, we were drawn to the example of
Christ's life as a child. As he himself grew in wisdom,
in stature, and in favor with God and man, he gave us
the pattern for wholesome, abundant life. He came that
we might have life and that we might have it more abun-

dantly. This begins even in childhood.

Thus Carolyn and I have written two music books—*A Child's Life in Song* and *Sing While You Grow.* These collections, composed of over 114 of our original songs, have developed through years of growing with our children. They contain insights often painfully gleaned in retrospect. Indeed, our own Christian parental pilgrimage has reinforced our conviction that if a child grows in all these areas, he is better prepared to like himself, to respect his fellowman, and to respond to God's love through Jesus Christ.

A second area in which we have consciously attempted to make our home a fresh and exciting creation is family camping. Our lives as husband and wife would have indeed been impoverished without this type of togetherness, We've tented with our children under our faithful Sears' canvas from Maine to Mexico, from the Gulf of Mexico to the desert wastes of the West. Some of our family's greatest lessons in patience, love, and acceptance were learned in the "Ted Williams Model" tent with the zip-down front door flap.

How beautiful the sunrise from Elephant Butte, New Mexico. How fragrant the pine bough mattress in New England's woods. How cool and inviting the rushing Colorado mountain stream as it played background music for a sumptuous banquet of crisp, fried rainbow trout and steaming coffee. How awe-inspiring the howling winds, tearing and tugging and uprooting our tent on the rocky promontory overlooking the Gulf of Saint Lawrence on Nova Scotia's Cabot Trail.

How humbling to emerge from a gritty tent, fully shaved, coiffured, and garbed to lead music for the W.M.U. annual meeting at the Southern Baptist Convention in Philadelphia. How utterly incredulous the looks on the faces of casually attired fellow campers. Eternal family memories are etched permanently upon our remembrances by camping trips.

The Long March

Like you, I'm sure, some of our most embarrassing, never to be forgotten family experiences have happened in church houses.

Never before had the church aisle seemed so long. It stretched before Carolyn as a parade route lined with spectators watching her pass in review.

Dragging our squirming, screaming four- and a half-year-old son, she marched from the church—blushing with embarrassment and anger. The minister's voice could be heard only faintly above the noise of their dramatic exit. I sat like some frozen, hoping not to be seen, Buddha in the choir director's chair on the platform.

It had started out to be such a lovely day. Mom Turnage, Carolyn's mother, who had been an invalid in our home for many months, was attending church for the first time; so to celebrate the occasion Carolyn had chosen to sit near the front of the church that she might fully enjoy the service. Neither of us could seem to concentrate upon the service, however. It had been such a mad rush to get all the family ready in time for Sunday School, then for Carolyn to teach the young people's class, and for me to lead the worship music. Racing through my mind were plans for maneuvering Mom Turnage and her metal walker into the car with ease and then help Carolyn fix dinner as quickly as possible for our hungry family. Instead of dropping cares for the moment and resting in quiet worship of God, we both found ourselves nervous and distracted.

Our son, seeming to sense Carolyn's disturbance, determined to make matters worse. He kept whistling aloud at intervals in spite of her frantic whispers to be quiet. Instead of drawing pictures on the church bulletin, he chose to mark inside the hymnal. She managed to regain the hymnal at the cost of much noise and looks of disapproval from neighbors in nearby pews. The pencil seemed to be ideal for a rocket ship so he sailed it into the air above his head—and the neighbors'! It landed in the center of the aisle. Frustrated because his rocket ship was out of reach, he insisted in a loud voice that Carolyn get it for him at once so he could sail it again.

Helplessly, viewing the situation from the platform, I realized that something had to be done immediately. The people sitting around my family were disturbed and unable to worship.

I signaled Carolyn with my eyes. She read the message.

"Get up, son, and walk quietly down the aisle. We're going outside," Carolyn whispered sternly.

"But I don't want to go," he replied belligerently. "I want to stay and sail my airplane."

"Get up and march down that aisle," she replied in no uncertain terms, accented with a quick jerk of his arm.

Recognizing that punishment was inevitable, he struggled to remain, but Carolyn overpowered him and began the long march to the church foyer and then outside.

Carolyn later commented that she felt she could never face the church family again or have the courage to take our boy inside the church. Such a crisis it was, that we both felt something positive and constructive must be done. As a family we sought the solution.

We decided we must not destroy the joy of worship with constant threats of physical punishment. We must help make "big church" worship a happy experience so that he would be glad when we said unto him, "Let us go into the house of the Lord."

But how? Carefully we scrutinized our own worship. Could he not sense our own spirit—our frequent lack of concentration, our occasional prayerless attitude, our meaningless participation at times in praise of God through song—our clock-watching when the service seemed too long—our unguarded caustic remarks about the service while coming home from church. If we ourselves did not worship God in spirit and in truth, how could we demand it of a young child?

The initial responsibility was ours as parents. Perhaps we could begin by teaching him something of the spirit of worship through our own family devotionals. They must be brief and geared to his understanding, permeated with unmistakable love of God and reverence for God.

Then too, we needed to realize that a child's attention span is brief, and busy hands are less disposed to mischief. We purchased a large writing tablet especially for church on Sunday. When the minutes seemed to drag and he needed a change, he opened the tablet and drew or wrote. It was his "church tablet" used especially for that occasion, and he prized it greatly.

And strangely enough, he began to listen better although his hands were busy drawing. Carolyn and I determined to comment pleasantly after church about specific aspects of the service—something in the sermon or about the music or the Scripture. Our son, to our surprise, commented too and evidently listened well—at times. "The preacher talked about the Old Testament today, Mother. I heard about the Old Testament in Sunday School."

The worship services became more meaningful to us. We found ourselves really praying, really singing, and really listening to God's message as interpreted by the pastor. Our son wasn't transformed into a motionless cherub, of course. He was still the same restless little four- and a half-year-old; but, nevertheless there was a difference. The dull dread within us at the thought of taking him into the worship services faded. We enjoyed worshiping together!

There was still a long march ahead to mature spiritual worship, but we started out together as a family and found joy in journeying.

Recorded for Eternity

Children are God's malleable gift—gold for us to fashion and to guide into paths of righteousness. How well I remember standing on tiptoe, and reaching to the top of our tall grandfather clock, feeling around for the key which would unlock its long, paneled door.

It was time to record another important event in Rhea family history. Already inside the door were inscribed our marriage date, the birthdays of our three children, and Carolyn's father's death.

Everyone gathered round, and even baby Meg watched happily from her playpen.

Carefully I slipped the key inside the clock door, turned the lock, and pulled it open. There we could see the ponderous weights hanging on the back. Painstakingly I scratched these words on the inside of the door:

"C³—Christian, Sept. 30, 1962."

Yes, our oldest son was now a Christian! A full-length movie of the entire experience was filmed on my mind during those brief moments. I recalled the surprise, even shock. I had felt when he made a public profession of his faith in Christ.

The baby was sick so I stayed home with her that morning while Carolyn taught her Sunday School class. Since we lived near the church, she was able to dash home to keep Meg while I hurried to church to sit with our two sons C³, almost eight and Randy, almost six.

We were quite late returning home from church. Carolyn would be concerned. The car stopped in our driveway, and Randy went flying into the house shouting, "Mother, C³ joined the church!"

"He did?" Carolyn exclaimed.

"Yes, Mother, I accepted Christ as Savior," C³ answered for himself as he walked into the kitchen.

"I'm glad, son," Carolyn managed to stammer as she hugged him. "This is a very important day for you."

As I viewed this scene I thought, "He isn't even eight yet. Does he really understand about salvation?" Always I had harbored secret reservations about young children joining the church. Now our own young son had already joined.

A little later I shared the full story with Carolyn.

"C³ listened attentively to the pastor's morning sermon, and when the invitation was given he turned to me and said, 'I'm going down the aisle, Daddy.'

" 'But son, are you sure that you know what you're doing?' I whispered.

" 'Yes, Daddy. I believe in Jesus as my Savior.'

" 'But son,' I protested, 'don't you want to wait until Mother can be here, too?'

" 'I must go now, Daddy,' he said, his hands gripping the pew in front.

" 'Then I want you to go, son,' I replied.

"He strode purposefully down the church aisle, dear," I continued, "took the pastor's hand, and made his profession of faith. Suddenly he seemed so mature. There's no way really to explain it. I only wish that you could have been there too."

"I'm glad you were the one with him, dear," Carolyn answered, "and I'm doubly glad that you feel he had a true salvation experience."

We pondered about it, talking it through with each other. Did it come about so young as a natural outgrowth? For years we had prayed in our family altar that our children might love God and come to know Jesus Christ as Savior. Had we not taken them to church, to Sunday School, to Vacation Bible School, read them Bible stories, helped them memorize Bible verses, encouraged them spiritually in every way we could?

Paul's words to young Timothy in 2 Timothy 3:15 took on deeper meaning for us. "And that from a child thou hast known the holy scriptures, which are able to make thee wise unto salvation through faith which is in Christ Jesus."

Friends rejoiced with us. One neighbor told C³, "Capture the joy of this experience, young man, and hold on to it for the rest of your life."

As friends dropped in the following week, our son's decision was the favorite topic of conversation; and they were eager to know the details and our own reaction. Suddenly I realized that other parents were just as vitally and personally concerned about their own children's salvation experience.

"I often wonder," one confided, "what it will be like when my child accepts Christ and what age she will be."

"My son is now eleven," another said, "and hasn't yet made a public profession of faith. I'm glad that you let C³ go ahead and do it when he really wanted to."

"When our son showed an interest, we planned with him when he would join the church," one mother said.

For an instant we almost envied her! I could picture her son handsomely and appropriately dressed for the dignified occasion. Then my mind relived our son striding down the aisle, hair unbrushed, shoes not polished, dressed helter-skelter in a worn-out plaid shirt and Sunday trousers instead of the usual white shirt and tie, sport coat and pants. Because the baby had been sick we were unable to supervise the boys' dressing for church that morning, and there was no time to send them back to change.

Would I have changed it even if I could? No. Claude evidently had a deeply moving personal encounter with God and felt compelled to do something about it.

He was no angel overnight! Our neighbors, his teacher, and we his parents could vouch for that! He was still our seven- and a half-year-old son to guide, to train, to teach, to love, to correct. But there *was* a tangible difference, and we now had a sure spiritual foundation upon which to build.

Even as he continued to disappoint us in many ways, so he would disappoint God and fall short of what is really expected of a Christian—even as we, his parents, disappoint God with our own weaknesses and failures. Ours would be the privilege these brief years to guide his spiritual growth and call to his remembrance the joy of his salvation.

I finished writing on the clock and rose to pray in the family circle. "Lord, we thank thee for thy Son Jesus Christ. We thank Thee for our son and his salvation experience. We thank thee for Randy and little Meg and pray that they too will grow toward an understanding of thy love through Christ."

The little ceremony was ended. I locked the clock and tucked the key away. Recorded inside the clock for generations to come was the fact that our young son had placed his trust in Jesus.

Surely that significant event had not gone unnoticed in heaven. It must have been entered into God's own journal of life—where it is recorded for eternity.

Middle C

"Mother, please teach me to play."

Our five-year-old daughter Meg was insistent about learning to play the piano. First, she had asked for piano lessons like those her friends were taking. Carolyn and I regretfully refused. At the time, our budget was stretched beyond the point of no return.

Meg, with her usual persistence, kept on pleading, "Mother, why don't *you* teach me to play the piano?" Carolyn was cornered. She couldn't refuse!

Being an amateur musician has its advantages. Impossible musical tasks and time-tested piano pedagogy methods are not considered binding. Carolyn devised her own method of teaching piano. In a matter-of-fact manner she reached for the masking tape, tore off a strip, stuck it on middle C, and proceeded with Meg's first lesson.

"This is middle C, Meg. This is where we begin."

Placing her thumb on middle C, Carolyn introduced our daughter to the adjacent white and black keys.

"Always remember middle C," Carolyn cautioned. "It will keep you from losing your way on the keyboard."

Faithfully Meg practiced each day for several weeks. Thumping her thumb on middle C, she would lustily sing out the other notes as she began to learn the musical notation for each.

While dusting one day, Carolyn noticed that Meg's grubby little hands had smudged and dirtied the masking tape. Impulsively and still while in a cleaning-up mood, my wife pulled the gummy tape off middle C.

Later that day I heard the distress call of a young female of the species. Meg ran crying into the kitchen where Carolyn was preparing lunch. Wringing her hands, she sobbed, "Mother! Mother! I've *lost* middle C! I've *lost* middle C!"

Our daughter's piano lessons taught us a lasting lesson about priorities in our lives. Jesus Christ is middle *C* on the Christian's keyboard of life. He is our starting point. He is both the "author and finisher of our faith." If we lose him as our middle C, we flounder in dissonance. With him we have fixed wholeness and completeness out of which can flow rivers of beauteous melody.[2]

A Certain Man Had Two Sons . . .

The story of the prodigal son has universal acceptance. In many of the forty-plus countries where I've given concerts, it has been revealing to see how the biblical account of a runaway son communicated. Each time I sang "The Penitent," the message crossed over the language barrier. In such diverse cultures as newly emerging Third World nations of East Africa and centuries old civilizations in the Far East, audiences understand the eternal pathos of a son coming to himself and returning to the patient, waiting love of his father.

I don't believe any family is ever prepared for the trauma and hurt of its own personal prodigal. Our younger son Randy, still in his teens, rebelled against the restrictions of our home. He ran away. Week after week we heard no word. As parents we literally wallowed in guilt, self-recrimination, and anguish. The hurt was so deep, the grief so intense that our very existence seemed to be suspended in a nightmarish dream sequence.

What had I done wrong? How had I failed as a father? There were no ready answers. Only the beat of a broken heart.

A friend sent Carolyn and me a copy of *My Utmost for His Highest* by Oswald Chambers. She suggested we read the selection from it entitled "The Patience of Faith." Chambers' words spoke to us.

> Patience is more than endurance. A saint's life is in the hands of God like a bow and arrow in the hands of an archer. God is aiming at something the saint cannot see, and He stretches and strains, and every now and again the saint says—"I cannot stand anymore." God does not heed, He goes on stretching till His purpose is in sight, then He lets fly. Trust yourself in God's hands. For what have you need of patience just now? Maintain your relationship to Jesus Christ by the patience of faith. "Though He slay me, yet will I wait for him." [3]

Carolyn and I learned from this that faith is not a pathetic sentiment. It is robust. Faith is confidence built on the fact that God is love. He loves our children much more than we as earthly parents ever can. Even though we could not see him just then, or understand what he was doing through this experience with Randy, we were sustained somehow.

We shared our deep need with members of our small prayer group at church. How they supported us in prayer. Week after week in the prayer group and day after day in their private prayer time they prayed for our Randy and for us. Through their prayers we kept unutterable trust in God, trust which never doubted he would somehow stand by us.

One Wednesday evening our prayer group had just finished. Once again they had specifically interceded for Randy and for us. There was a noise at the door of the prayer room, an embarrassed clearing of the throat, and a rather subdued voice croaked, "Mother . . ."

Our prodigal son had returned from the far country. Dirty and disheveled. Drawn homeward and churchward in answer to prayer.[3]

"For this my son was dead but is alive again . . . he was lost but now is found."

With My Song I Will Praise Him

"Sing While You Grow"

Sing, sing, sing while you grow.
Grow in wisdom, Learn and recall,
Grow in stature, straight and tall.
Grow in favor with God.
Grow in favor with man.
And sing while you grow.[4]*

CAROLYN AND CLAUDE RHEA

6 When They Ring Those Golden Bells

"For this corruptible must put on incorruption, and this mortal must put on immortality" (1 Cor. 15:53).

Grandpa and the Woodpecker

"No, Grandpa's *not* dead! He's not!"

A belligerent little four-year-old stormed angrily after waking, overhearing our frantic early morning telephone calls. We were making hasty arrangements to leave for Florida following the news of the death of my wife's father.

Could a child of four already have frightening ideas about death? Could our present explanation possibly affect his emotional and spiritual growth? Just how could we explain death to our four-year-old son?

C^3 and Grandpa had always been so close. It was almost as if the "child" in the elder reached out in understanding response as they shared fresh joys and discoveries: the little bags of candy, balloons, and goodies; holding C^3 in his arms to watch the trains with engines on the track in front of the big country store where Grandpa worked, the Boy Scout tent long before C^3 was big enough to enjoy it, building countless birdhouses for every conceivable perch in the year . . . birds! That was it! How explain death so a child could understand? Grandpa had already done it for us!

Remember Jerry the woodpecker? Carolyn had laughed in good-natured disbelief when her father began to tell C³ of Jerry, a little red-headed woodpecker who came when he called.

"C³, Son, you must learn to call him, too."

So C³ and Grandpa would stand on the back porch while Grandpa gave a shrill whistle and with cupped hands called out, "Hey, Jerry, way down yonder in the moss-covered swamp, come here! We have some biscuits for you!"

As he continued to call, a little answering "peck-peck-peck" could be heard on the tin roof of the adjacent garage.

Then grandson and elder would toss cold biscuit crumbs into the grass. With a quick swoop Jerry would dart into the open area and greedily snatch up the crumbs. Gaining confidence, he'd perch on his favorite fence post, his perky little head shining like a red patch upon the faded gray denim wood.

C³ and Grandpa would laugh with sheer delight! Then our son would manfully try to call Jerry just as Grandpa did.

This unique friendship continued for nearly two years, and C³ eagerly anticipated each visit to Grandpa's so he could see Jerry.

One early spring day when we were visiting Carolyn's mother and dad, C³ ran immediately to the porch and called for Jerry. He called again and again, but this time Jerry didn't come. Grandpa, having welcomed us, started for the porch to join C³.

"Jerry's dead," Mom Turnage told us. "We're going to miss him. Strange thing about that bird," she continued, "seemed almost as if he knew he was goin' to die and came here to be with us. Old and tired, I guess. He perched on the post beneath the birdhouse for a day or so. Rained and turned cold, so he might've caught pneumonia. We found him dead on the ground beside the post so we buried him in the pet cemetery. He was almost like part of the family."

Glancing through the kitchen door, we could see Grandpa carefully pull up his big porch chair and gently lift C³ into his lap.

Quietly he began to tell him of Jerry's death. "Son, Jerry's not going to be with us anymore. You see, the Lord took Jerry home. He'd grown old and tired and then one day he got so sick that God just thought it best to take Jerry on with him."

He continued with the story, telling C³ how Jerry came there to be with them when he died. Then he showed him Jerry's little grave in the pet cemetery where Carolyn and her sister had buried their pets throughout the years.

"Jerry has a little family down in the swamps, son. Mrs. Jerry came up a few times for biscuit crumbs and even brought her little woodpeckers. So you see, Jerry's little family is still with us."

Wasn't it strange that a man of fifty-eight would take the time to explain the death of a bird so carefully to a three- and a half-year-old? Carolyn and I smiled worldly-wise "adult" smiles, but C³ seemed satisfied with Grandpa's explanation.

"The Lord took Jerry home, Mudder. He got sick 'n died. But he left us some *little* woodpeckers! Aren't we glad!"

. . . Gently Carolyn lifted C³ into her arms and looking into his big questioning eyes, quietly said, "Yes, son, Grandpa *is* dead. He was tired and sick, and God thought it best to take Grandpa home with him. Do you remember Jerry? And what Grandpa told you about his leaving us?"

As C³ verbally recounted his memories of Jerry, he seemed to arrive at his own childish acceptance of death. It was not frightening. God was in it all, and God was good.

Before leaving Florida, we drove out to the cemetery to Pop Turnage's fresh grave with its array of flowers. Pointing it out to C³, we explained that Grandpa was buried there.

"Yes, I know," he responded. "But Grandpa's not *really* there. He's home with God."

His bright assurance comforted us, and our own faltering faith was strangely renewed.

Mom Turnage

Carolyn's mother, Mom Turnage, moved into our home shortly after Pop Turnage's death. For four years her presence was a benediction. She had a personal ministry, it seemed, especially tailored for each member of our family. How can we ever possibly measure the depth and breadth of the love of flowers and all things growing she taught our children? Her own love for shrubs and flowers and trees rubbed off on our young, impressionable children. Happily they helped her prepare the soil; carefully they tucked in the green plants; ecstatically they rejoiced when flowers bloomed. Grandma's day lilies, periwinkles, amaryllis, four-o'clocks, shrimp plants, and other old-fashioned perennials proved to be a source of joy and beauty.

And her vegetable garden was a continuing lesson about the cycle of life: planting, tending, bearing, dying. Especially memorable were the football-sized cantaloupes the children harvested. And what a struggle they had fending off the dog, for Mimi delighted in digging up and eating the delicate carrots and radishes! (It was at Grandma's insistence that we had gone to the S.P.C.A. and redeemed our mutt.)

Grandma's ability with hammer and saw was legendary. Indisputably, she was the guiding light for helping the boys plan and construct their rough-hewn fort. Singlehandedly, she salvaged left-over lumber from construction projects in the neighborhood. Doggedly, she defended the boys' grandiose plans for erecting their stolid structure. (I must admit the ragged end result didn't exactly match the studied architecture of our Houston home!) But what memories were entwined with the boys' blistered hands!

How priceless to partake of matchless family recipes from South Georgia which Mom Turnage painstakingly prepared for us: cornbread dressing at Thanksgiving, blackberry cobbler, mile-high country biscuits, hush puppies, corn pone, delicate custard pudding. How graciously—how warmly she served as senior hostess in our home.

But then cancer hit her hard. The bloom left. Activity declined. She fought back and slowly won. But then hardening of the arteries developed. Personality changed. Depression. Forgetfulness. Gradually, Carolyn and I found we had another child in our home—a child with an aging adult body—a child with adult attitudes and feelings—an adult who was a parent living in the home of her children, who were also responsible, adult parents.

This was a difficult time for each one of us. Carolyn was forced into the fragmented role of wife, daughter, mother, teacher, part-time college student. The pressures of my profession as music dean and later as administrative vice-president fought for my attention and time. The path of easiest resistance for me was to "bail out" and to escape facing up honestly to the heightening crisis in our home.

Our children, with inherent insights, attempted to win their point of view in confrontations by pitting parents against grandparent. The idealism of Christian faith was being tested and strained at the seams by increasing tensions.

Our family with three generations living under one roof was in danger of permanent scars. We experienced deep-seated guilt as we attempted to share feelings as husband and wife with a parent in the home. Mom Turnage could not grasp what we were trying to say or do. She began a slow withdrawal into her shell of self. Invisible barriers were erected at the door of her room. Sounds of silence were deafening at mealtimes. Open rupture of relationships was imminent. Somehow the communication gap couldn't be bridged.

Then, without warning, cancer struck again. Radium implants followed radical surgery. Extensive hospitalization eroded and finally ate up meager life savings. The disease ravaged her body. Diabetic-like comas unpredictably swept Mom Turnage into periods of unconsciousness.

It became increasingly evident we could not bring her back to our home. The doctors strongly urged a convalescent center near the hospital for necessary medical monitoring. Carolyn and I made one of the toughest decisions of our marriage—Mom Turnage must be admitted to a rest home. In her generation, this was something that was just not done. We too, held the conviction that Christians should welcome aging parents, regardless of the circumstances, into their homes—should love and tenderly care for them during times of need. Yet, we were trapped in an inescapable milieu. With our own three children demanding more and more time and with Carolyn forced to return to teaching and further college preparation in order to help pay the staggering medical bills, we had to

WHEN THEY RING THOSE GOLDEN BELLS

weigh seriously the doctors' suggestions for extended care of Mom Turnage in a convalescent home.

The decision made, I tiptoed into the hospital room and found Carolyn gently brushing her mother's hair, attempting to untangle the snarls and restore a personal dignity robbed by illness. "Mom Turnage," I whispered, "your doctors say you need some extended nursing care. They recommend we move you to the Medicenter Convalescent Home for a few weeks."

"Yes, Mother," said Carolyn, "it's the best facility in Houston. What do you think?"

Slowly, without any sign of recognition whatsoever, a regal saint closed her vacant eyes, turned her back upon her children and faced the blank hospital wall. Silence.

We attempted unsuccessfully to gain her assent. On the appointed day we moved her. The attendants wheeled a silent, wasted, withdrawn, greatly beloved lady to the waiting ambulance. She was whisked to the rest home. There cheerful, trained attendants tenderly ministered to her needs. The best of medical science was marshaled in her behalf.

Soon it was Christmas. We brought her presents. Our family stood around the bed and sang "Silent Night, Holy Night." Mom Turnage kept her eyes tightly closed—her lips sealed—her face steadfastly turned toward the wall. Our presence was not acknowledged. We were earthly. Her corruptible was already putting on the incorruptible.

"Merry Christmas, Grandma!" shouted the children. No reply was forthcoming.

"Why doesn't Grandma answer?" questioned Randy. A hot tear slid down his chubby cheek.

"Grandma's resting," Carolyn said softly. We slipped out of stony silence.

The jangling of a telephone awakened me. I struggled

through the dark bedroom and answered. An impersonal voice of a nurse said, "Mrs. Turnage died in her sleep early this morning. Please come to the home when you can. Arrangements must be made." Grandma had quietly, unobtrusively slipped away. How very much like her to wait until the day *after* Christmas.

Mom Turnage took her long-awaited first plane ride back home to Florida for interment. There she rests near some Spanish moss-draped live oak trees. A simple stone announces her name and asserts her faith: "The Lord is my Shepherd." It's peaceful there at Mount Pleasant Cemetery.

Death

Death is the dividing line between the numerator of present life and the unknown denominator of eternity. Only through becoming a part of the division process can I discover for myself the ratio—that full relationship which God has perceived all along. Death is not a terror to be feared but a kindly instrument wielded in the hands of God by which He brings a mortal into the joy of His immortal presence.[1]

With My Song I Will Praise Him

"When They Ring Those Golden Bells"

There's a land beyond the river,
That we call the sweet forever,
And we only reach that shore by faith's decree;
One by one we'll gain the portals,
There to dwell with the immortals,
When they ring those golden bells for you and me.

CHORUS

Don't you hear those bells now ringing?
Don't you hear the angels singing?
'Tis the glory hallelujah Jubilee.
In that far-off sweet forever,
Just beyond the shining river,
When they ring those golden bells for you and me.

—DION DE MARBELLE

I joined the army and saw the world. There's T/5 Claude Rhea in front of St. Peter's, Rome, Italy (1946).

"Because you come to me with nought save love . . ." *Carolyn and I on our wedding day, August 26, 1951*

Student missionaries to the Hawaiian Islands (the summer of '49)—Carolyn (front, third from left), yours truly (second row, third from left)

A recent family portrait—our children, standing, are (left to right) Randy, Meg, and Claude (C³).

A Christian singer's dream come true—to present a sacred concert at the Garden Tomb in Jerusalem (1967)

Fellowshipping with Japanese students in Tokyo (1969)

One of my greatest joys has been to serve and worship with
Christians all over the globe. Here I talked with leaders from
Nigeria and Guatemala at the Baptist World Alliance (1965).

Here I was with Dr. Lewis Smith, medical missionary and my
accompanist, in the interior of Luzon, Philippines.

What an honor to work with Dr. Billy Graham during his Birmingham Crusade of 1972!

C³ and I about to board a boat for a canal tour of Amsterdam, Holland

In concert at the National Theater of Korea

With two internationally known artists, Doc Severinson of the "Tonight Show" (left) and Andre Previn . . .

. . . and with Norma Zimmer of the "Lawrence Welk Show" and Gene Bartlett, composer

Mayor Louie Welch commissioning me as Houston's "Singing Ambassador to the Orient"

Dr. Leslie S. Wright, president of Samford University, presenting me a special Birmingham Festival of Arts Award

Back in 1961, Dr. Walter Pope Binns, president, and I at Achievement Day for William Jewell College

7 Ask of Me . . .

"Ask of me, and I will give thee the nations for thine inheritance, and the uttermost parts of the earth for thy possession" (Ps. 2:8, ASV).

My missionary journey had its beginning in a Sunbeam Band in my home church in Missouri. Faithful women of the church gave of their time and talents to instruct us children about missions around the globe. Far countries came alive. *National Geographic* scenes were fleshed-out in the persons of visiting missionaries. Calendar of Prayer objects became real-live people who spoke and communicated and let us hold objects of art from strange cultures.

During my high school days and while I was overseas in the Army of Occupation, my interest in foreign missions expanded. I sent down permanent taproots of concern for missions even as I worked with Christian youth groups in war-ravaged Germany.

My introduction to Psalm 2:8 proved to be the key to unlatch and to swing open my life to God's leadership. It happened in Liberty, Missouri.

Even after thirty years my initial encounter with Eugenia Lake Kellersberger is as fresh as this morning's newspaper. She was a commanding personality—infectious with her sheer joy of living. She swept into our Missionary Fellow-

ship Group at William Jewell College for the 7:00 A.M.
weekly meeting. No one can ever quite shake the encompassing, outgoing love of this statuesque missionary
stateswoman. She and her missionary doctor husband had
pioneered Christian medical missions in the Congo. They
founded and nurtured the American Mission to the Lepers.

Back in America on furlough during 1947, she was
speaking to interested groups across the South and Mid-
west. Mrs. Kellersberger gave us a life's verse that day—
one of God's greatest missionary promises. She had us
commit to memory in that early morning hour. "Ask of
me and I will give you the nations for your inheritance
and the uttermost parts of the earth for your possession"
(Ps. 2:8). Can you fathom such a far-reaching promise?
God has said we have but to ask and he will surely give
us the nations of the world for our inheritance and the
uttermost part of this earth for our possession!

I claimed Psalm 2:8 that day as one of God's great
promises for my life. Through these intervening decades,
he has heard and honored his Word. Let me share with
you how.

Ask of Me . . . Hawaii

The Paradise of the Pacific . . . the land of flowers and
of palms, of blue skies and rainbows . . . the land of cool,
fertile valleys.

Fourteen of us Baptist Student Missionaries were chosen
to represent our fellow Baptist students in Hawaii during
the summer of 1949. Eager and radiant, we stepped across
the threshold of this land and became a part of its heartbeat
for seven glorious weeks. Behind that curtain of beauty
were some 525,000 people, of whom over 90 percent did

not know Christ.

At Kokokahi, Hawaii's "Little Ridgecrest," we had our first opportunity to meet the Christians of the islands. We saw the happiness that lighted their faces; they, too, knew Christ and the life that brings peace and joy and happiness. Their testimonies and their dynamic Christian living provided a challenge to Christians everywhere.

The Buddhists of Hawaii believe that each year in July the spirits of the dead return to earth. They place food on the graves that the spirits might have something to eat. To entertain these spirits, they have *bon* dances in which thousands of Japanese, young and old, ignorant and educated, participate.

Upon asking several young Japanese who attend these dances to explain their meaning, we received answers like this: "We don't really know what it's all about." Some attend because they were brought up in Buddhist customs; some still participate because they enjoy it. The older generation of Japanese is the one who still clings in firm faith to strict Buddhism.

Upon asking, "What about this Buddha you worship? Is he just your symbol for a God or is he a real personal God who loves you?" we received answers to this effect: "No, we don't know Buddha. He's just there." How could they possibly KNOW a god of wood?

Assigned to different churches on different islands, all fourteen of us were busy in Vacation Bible School work. Arseino, a little Primary boy (we called them Primaries back then), symbolized to us the privilege and opportunity we had of sharing Christ with boys and girls of all races.

We could not seem to remember his name, so we found ourselves calling him "Arsenic." Arsenic learned to love the Bible through our Bible study each day. He had learned to find the Lord's Prayer, John 3:16, Psalm 23, and almost any Bible reference, and was outstanding in sword drills.

The last day of Bible School, clasping a dime tightly in his little hand, Arsenic came over to us. In his Pidgin English, he said, "See money I brought? Me want Bible take home with me." Carolyn marked passages about the plan of salvation, and with a prayer in her heart, sent a Bible by little Arsenic into a Filipino home that did not know Christ.

Many decisions were made for Christ in youth revivals held in two of the Honolulu churches. Through prayer, visitations, personal works, the Christian message in song, personal testimonies, and the simple presentation of God's love through Christ, we tried to point many the way to that abundant life which Christ gives.

One student, thinking of the paganism and of the great need of Christ existing in Hawaii, eagerly exclaimed to one of the island Christians, "Aren't they *hungry* for the gospel and for Christ out here?" "How can they be hungry," he replied, "for what they have never tasted?"

These words pierced our hearts as we thought of those thousands of people in Hawaii who do not know the God who gave them the beauty of their rainbows and flowers, and who do not know his great love through Christ and happiness within his will.

Ask of Me . . . Panama

During the late 1950s the San Blas Islands, scattered a few miles up and down the coast of Panama, still hosted some of the world's most primitive spots. Evil spirits were still feared and worshiped. Witch doctors still practiced psychosomatic medicine. As our single-engine plane buzzed the island of Aligandi, I could see thatched huts dotting the tiny mound of sand and coral. Myriads of brightly clad Cuna Indians ran to the center of the settlement, gazed skyward and waved excitedly. The bush pilot banked the plane sharply, cut back the throttle, and glided in smoothly for a perfect landing on the waving sea-grass runway. The faded "airport" wind sock waved proudly in its tattered splendor in the trade wind.

As the propeller wound down to a whining halt, a bespectacled, chubby, smiling face greeted me. It was the fabled Lonnie Iglesias. During his lifetime, this living legend had been a smuggler, businessman, senator in the Panamanian legislature, and spokesman for the entire Cuna tribe. Now he stood at his tallest vocational stature—a lay Baptist preacher and servant of his people. As we walked to the dock, I fell into step with him, basking in the warmth of a genuine human being. The next sight shook me up! Our boat. It was a long, hollowed-out log with outriggers. I gingerly stepped down into this rough-hewn craft and thoroughly expected to be baptized beneath the Caribbean waves. Much to my surprise it floated. The Indian boatmen skillfully and adroitly paddled us seaward. Within the hour we beached at Aligandi. A slightly seasick, former Army man gratefully stepped out onto firm land.

The next week was a virtual treasure chest full of new discoveries. I lived in the Iglesias' concrete-block home. As their guest I had free run of the entire island. Each morning the day's activities began with the sound of laughter and fully clothed, splashing communal bathers in the deep blue waters off the nearby coral reef. The pungent odor of smoke from each hut's cooking pit hung suspended on the turgid morning air. Dugout canoes plied back and forth to the mainland. San Blas women paddled up nearby rivers with empty calabash water holders. Once beyond the reach of the tides, they dipped up fresh, sweet water into their gourds and headed back to their island home. This was a daily chore unless hindered by squalls.

One morning several young natives began a series of dives deep beneath the sparkling waters off the reef. After long intervals they splashed through the surface, fighting for air, but triumphantly holding above their heads spindley, squirming lobsters. Promptly these delicacies were plunged into containers of boiling sea water. After the lobsters turned the proper shade of blushing red, we devoured these gourmet morsels until our hunger was satisfied.

There is no darkness quite as enveloping as that in a San Blas village. Once the power generator is quieted for the night, the electricity dissipates, and the lights gradually fade. The black velvet ensues. Soon little coconut oil lamps began sputtering in individual huts. Lonnie Iglesias and I walked unnoticed through the shadows. In the tribal council hut in the center of the community sat a wizened old man. He held a nose flute in his lap. He chanted in the strange, guttural Cuna tongue. He moved with the dignity of the decades as he placed the flute to his nostril and blew into the tubular instrument. The plaintive melody strangely akin to Chinese music floated on the night air. An epic tale of the tribe was being passed down from the elder statesman to the neophyte, much in the tradition of Beowulf tales.

That night as I drifted into sleep, I heard the beating of wings on the chicken-wire mesh stretched across the windows. I stirred under the mosquito net swathed over my bed and thought it strange that birds would be attempting to fly into the room. Lonnie told me the next morning what those birds were—vampire bats!

The capstone of my visit to the San Blas Islands was my concert in the church and the reception which followed. The men all sat on my right—the women on the left. A droning fan lazily stirred the tepid air in the church. A few moths and indolent mosquitos bravely attempted to buzz about. The women were dressed in the traditional *mola*. These indigenous costumes were made of multiple layers of appliqué cloth, cut and individually designed. In the women's noses were gold rings. Heavy, golden ornaments stretched their pierced ear lobes into grotesque shapes. With their gaily printed head scarves, they delicately fanned themselves with unison motions. I became so fascinated with their choreographed fanning that I almost forgot the words to my songs.

At the conclusion of the concert, the chief of Aligandi invited me to a reception. As guest of honor I was plied with gifts of mola, a hand-carved boat for my children, musical instruments hand-fashioned from bamboo, pelican wing pinions, and even a whistle devised from a tatooed human shin bone and pitch. I was solemnly renamed "Little White Nephew."

The culminating act was the offering of a coconut shell filled to the brim with a Cuna drink—a potion made from corn. Earlier in the day, women in the tribe chewed corn off the cobs, thoroughly salivated it, and then spit the chewed corn into bowls. This liquid was then mixed with sugar cane and water. It was simmered over a low fire for the remainder of the day. Every eye in the tribal council ring was upon me. I took the cup, saluted the group, thanked them for the privilege of being in their midst, offered a quick, silent prayer for a strong stomach, and heartily quaffed the sickly sweet corn drink. Smacking my lips in the locally expected manner, I made comment about the refreshing quality of the native delicacy. (After all, it was quite a long swim back to Panama.)

Then feigning tiredness from the strenuous concert, I excused myself from the group. I was not prepared to counteract the corn drink medically. All the medication I had brought along with me was a large, economy-sized bottle of *Pepto-Bismol.* Without even a second thought I drank it down. *Prayerfully. Completely.*

Six weeks later the slow-acting liver virus struck. My billirubin count was out of sight. I had contacted some sort of liver infection. The doctor described it as a rare type of hepatitis. Yet—it was worth it all. For how often in this world does a person receive the signal honor of having his name changed to "Little White Nephew"?

Ask of Me . . . Rüschlikon

This was a congregational song service that was different. A German concert pianist, Dr. Herbert Dobiey, was giving a firm Brahmsian flavor to the piano accompaniment. Gerald Barnes, organist of Bloomsbury Central Baptist Church in London, was at the console playing the hymns in a meticulous, somewhat detached British style. The congregation was made up of eighty church musicians from all over Europe. They were gathered at the Baptist Seminary in Rüschlikon, Switzerland, for the first European Baptist Music Conference. There was a sense of expectancy during these early June days of 1959. Baptist music history was being made.

This was the first international meeting ever attempted by European Baptist church musicians and musically minded pastors. The express purpose of the congress was for investigating both common and unique problems facing the Baptist bodies on the European continent. Christian musicians had traveled from afar to share ideas and ideals. A climate of free and tolerant dialogue was being sought.

What a difficult task faced us. Each country's representatives brought with them strong nationalistic feeling, varying cultures and backgrounds, wounds and hurts incurred in two world wars, and preconceived ideas about music methodology. Could we possibly overcome all of these barriers and find a common meeting ground for understanding?

As I gave the downbeat for the hymn, words welled up from multiple hearts and found musical expression in divergent tongues: *"Gesegnet sei das Band das uns im Herrn vereint!" "Benditos sean los lazos que nos unen" "Ljuut Karleksbandet ar som Dristi Lemmar band" "Siam Figli D'un Solo Riscatto."* "Blest be the tie that binds our hearts in Christian love." The wooden rafters of the chapel at Rüschlikon rang with this message of hope and unity and Christian oneness. This was the key to understanding one another—our hymnody.

In the days which followed, we came to many an impasse. Some positions were frozen by centuries of tradition. Others stubbornly refused to see "new light." But one thing the Rüschlikon conference did achieve. In spite of vast differences, constructive efforts by Baptists to glorify God through church music were begun. Various national groups which had begun the music conference as unlike fractions had been added together to make a larger whole. As Baptist church musicians we found a common denominator—God's love through Christ. Love neutralized our major differences. Together as one brotherhood we could honor God. "Blest be the tie that binds our hearts in Christian love."

Ask of Me . . . Spain

The small Peugeot car bounced over the cobblestone

streets of Madrid. In the early, predawn hours, the yellow
fog lights of the missionary's compact auto cast eerie shadows on the serrated pavement. We skidded to a biting
halt on the damp gravel of the road's apron. There was
a single light burning in a second-story room of the faded
stucco building. We softly closed the car door and stumbled
through the rising mist into the dank, dark hallway. A
door opened on the landing, allowing garish rays of light
to permeate the blackness. A Spanish Baptist pastor mo-
tioned silently for us to come up into his pastorium apart-
ment. Hot mugs of steaming, dark roast coffee were awaiting as tokens of his best Castillian welcome.

After brief greetings and exchanges of pleasantries, the
pastor, through the interpreter, asked if I would like to
"see" his church. Mustering up my best Spanish, I said,
"Si." The light in the hallway was extinguished. We felt
our way back down the stairwell and into a small vestibule.
One of the missionaries was posted as guard at the outer
doorway leading to the street. The Spanish pastor, Missionary Joe Mefford, and I moved quietly through the
hallway to our right.

As my eyes adjusted to the grayness, a door, its facing,
and a slip of worn paper began to come into focus. I stared
in disbelief. The church was "sealed." The story seemed
to literally cascade from the lips of the pastor. He related
how one morning the government troops came during the
worship hour and herded out of that little building the
brave band of evangelicals that met there for divine services. By order of the local military commandment, a "seal"
was placed over the entranceway—officially closing the
church to worship and declaring it illegal and off limits.

The charge? Disturbing the peace. The accuser? A local
representative of the state church. I examined the "seal"
more closely. During the three years since it had been

affixed, moisture in the air had gradually loosened the glue. Now all that kept the Baptists out of their meeting house was a "seal" temporarily posted with two rusty thumbtacks—and, of course, the power of the entire Spanish army.

The pastor spoke more softly now. "Would you like to go inside my church?" I nodded affirmatively. He deftly pulled out one of the tacks. The "seal" slid to half-mast. The door creaked open. We stepped inside the sanctuary. Dust was on the pews. The hymn boards still mutely announced the numbers sung that fateful morning. A holy silence enveloped us. We held a belated worship service. The pastor prayed, oh so poignantly. The missionary read Scripture. The Spanish pastor turned to me and requested that I sing.

"But please, senor," he whispered, "not too loudly, or the police may come—and you will be a 'guest' of our government for the rest of this year." I struggled with the lump that rose in my throat. What should be sung in such a moment? I chose a simple Negro spiritual—a melody with plaintive simplicity—a timeless message that bespoke the first-century brand of Christianity so implicit in Spanish Baptists. "Lord, I want to be a Christian in my heart! in my heart! Lord, I want to be like Jesus in my heart!"

Tears coursed down our cheeks. The song was finished. The brief worship was over. The sound of silence once again descended upon the dusty little church. With somber hearts we left the place of encounter. The door was reluctantly closed. The "seal" replaced. Then it happened. A solitary, lone thought began its swelling crescendo. It filled my mind and engulfed my entire being. In spite of trials, tribulations, and persecution for righteousness sake, *the church is still alive and well! GOD'S CHURCH IS TRIUMPHANT!*

Ask of Me . . . Indonesia

Phnom Penh

The trip from Bombay to Rangoon had been singularly uneventful. The jet droned hypnotically. I slept fitfully, read endless reams of outdated magazines, and visited in fractured French with the group of priests sitting across the aisle from me. They were traveling to a missionary assignment in Cambodia. The pilot's voice broke into the travel-sedated atmosphere of the cabin. "Ladies and gentlemen, may I have your attention please? Fasten your seat belts. We will be landing in a very few moments at Phnom Penh."

In 1963 the capital of Cambodia was not exactly a household word. I suppose many had heard of the famous ruins at Angkor-wat on the outskirts of the city, but for most of us, this was a place passed by and relegated for the most part to the archeologists and history buffs.

I dozed off in a state of seminirvana awaiting the squeal of the Air France jet's tires at touchdown. Instead of deceleration, however, there was a sudden burst of power! The pilot gave full throttle. A hefty infusion of kerosene caused the mighty machine to roar and shriek and shudder to sudden life. Our heads were thrust back and glued into the seats. We were experiencing mechanical difficulties in the landing gear.

The plane circled for a full fifteen minutes while fuel was jettisoned. Instructions were given to prepare for an emergency crash landing. I glanced over at my friends, the French priests. They were busy counting their beads and saying prayers. Not wanting to be outdone and certainly feeling the need to do something religious, I reached into my coat pocket. All I could find was an old offering envelope with the 8 Point Record System printed on it! I

began reciting: "Present. On Time . . ." Just as I read
"Brought Bible," we crunched down and began a long,
interminable skid across the foam-layered runway. The
left wing tip dipped. We sped diagonally toward the waiting
jungle. The landing gear plowed deeply into the softer
soil bordering the concrete strip. This broke the plane's
onrushing momentum. The careening jet came to a merciful halt. Quickly we evacuated the cabin and ran toward
the terminal.

For two days all of us passengers were guests of Air
France in Phnom Penh. The whole scene was strangely
reminiscent of a late, late Humphrey Bogart movie. The
old hotel left over from French colonial days. The dim
10-watt light bulb in a frayed, dangling socket. Plaster
cracked on the walls. A ceiling fan which barely stirred
the humid air. The balcony overlooked the busy thor-
oughfare of the capital city. Pedicabs rushed pell-mell
through packed humanity. Numbers of the slats in the
shuttered doorway were broken. Insects, both imagined
and real, paraded across the bed's muslin sheets. How
welcome the announcement the next morning that a relief
plane would arrive that afternoon from Paris and convey
us on to Djakarta.

Indonesia

The twinkling lights of Djakarta reminded me of innumerable miniature fireflies scattered across the black velvet
darkness of the island of Java. A contingency of missionaries awaited me outside the custom's area. They had been
meeting each plane arriving in Indonesia for the past two
days.

My welcome to Djakarta was tempered by the news that
we would depart early the next morning for Semarang.
I was informed by my host, "It's over two hundred miles

to Central Java. We'll have to leave no later than 4:00
A.M." "That's just four hours from now," I protested. "Why
get up so early just to drive two hundred miles? Isn't my
concert at 9:00 tomorrow evening?"

Sixteen hours later a weary tenor, his medical-missionary
accompanist, and the dusty driver arrived in Semarang.
It might have clocked only two hundred miles horizontally
from Djakarta to Central Java, but it most certainly was
eighteen hundred miles up and down over those nonexistent Indonesian roads.

There was no time for a shower. No time to warm up
vocally. No time to gargle. Just a few minutes to scrape
off a day's growth of beard, anoint myself with my favorite
after shave lotion, and jump into my summer tuxedo.

The concert hall was a typical Southeast Asian one. It
was "air-conditioned." The air blew in one side and out
the other. Street noises were an integral part of the concert.
Dogs barked. Children cried. Vendors came into the hall
and sold sandwiches and cold drinks. People stood up,
walked about, and visited with friends. A peddler came
in and began offering live chickens for sale. He had these
clucking beauties trussed on a long bamboo pole.

I thought that I surely had undergone the ultimate in
audience challenge. But I was mistaken. The evening's
piece de resistance was yet to come. Forty-five minutes into
the concert, I heard a new, distinctive sound. Far off in
the distance was the unmistakable wail of motorcycle
sirens. They came closer and closer. Then they stopped.
Right in front of the auditorium. The audience turned to
watch the action. For the first time all evening a quietness
prevailed.

As the shrill decibels of the sirens on the twelve motorcycles subsided, two jeep loads of troops skidded to a halt
in the loose gravel of the driveway. Fully armed and hel-

meted soldiers jumped out and fanned across the back
of the theater. They stood at port arms. An ancient
Mercedes-Benz with an Indonesian flag flying from a standard on the front fender glided into view. A chauffeur
opened the back door. Out stepped an army general. He
was in full-dress uniform with medals and all. He literally
clinked down to the front row. The entire audience stood
rigidly at attention until the general and his military
attaché were seated. I leaned over to Dr. Keith Parks, my
interpreter, and whispered, "Keith, what shall I tell this
guy?"

"Claude," he replied, "say anything you want to, I'll
take care of it in the translation." Keith must have done
just that. For as I smiled and bowed low to the general,
and greeted him, he returned my greeting. The concert
proceeded to its conclusion. The general and his retinue
made their august departure. I thought the incident was
closed.

But the next day, the missionaries received a phone call
from General Sarbini's attaché, requesting that we come
and have tea with the commandant at his home. In Central
Java when the military leader of the area requests that
you have tea, you have tea! We were challenged by several
cordons of guards before we reached the driveway of the
large home liberated from the Dutch several years earlier
by government forces.

The general greeted us at the door and invited us into
the beautifully appointed reception area. We chatted at
length, slowing down only long enough for our interpreters
to frame our thoughts in each other's language. At the
appropriate time, General Sarbini clapped his hands, mo-
tioned toward the silken curtains and snapped out some
commands. Almost immediately the curtains parted and
servants laden with silver trays came into the room. How

precariously the silver tea pots and creamer and sugar bowl were perched. The servants in deference to Indonesian custom came into our presence half-crouched, making sure their heads were lower than the seated master of the household. I finally decided that they must be running on radar. Silently, almost gravely, they poured the tea and offered us Javanese delicacies.

Three times this ritual took place. Three times we were offered refreshments. Then the general stood. That was our cue. The visit was over. As a final gesture, General Sarbini presented me with an autographed portrait of himself. He walked with us to the entranceway. Once again I thought the contact had ended.

Dr. Lewis Smith and I left for our two-week concert tour of Indonesia. As we were preparing to leave the country for Malaysia, the missionaries shared with us the sequel to the Semarang incident.

Several days after our concert, the general's attache phoned our Baptist missionaries and requested that a class in conversational English be organized for the military headquarters' staff. General Sarbini wanted to learn to speak English. The request was, of course, honored. It was an answer to prayer. For over eight years the missionaries had been praying for an opportunity to share the gospel with this strategic leader and his staff. A wide-open door was afforded for contact on a permanent basis with the general.

For over two years the English conversation and reading class met one day a week. General Sarbini and his leading officers participated faithfully. Then the general was transferred to Djakarta and the classes ended.

I had almost forgotten about the concert in Semarang and the meeting with the general. But on the morning of October 1, 1965, I was abruptly reminded of the incident.

I was startled to read the newspaper headlines "Communists Attempt Coup in Indonesia." During the night of September 30, 1965, the Indonesian Communists attempted to seize control of the nation. Many leading military leaders were arrested and/or assassinated in their homes. The national radio station was overrun. All traffic was paralyzed. Communications with the outside world ceased. The power of the central government teetered on the brink of collapse. Two powerful military leaders of the central government escaped. One was General Suharto, now President of Indonesia. The other one was the man I like to call "my general," General Sarbini.

He was reading in bed late at night, as was his custom. He heard the barking of his dog and the sound of vehicles down the street. He sensed immediate danger and jumped out his bedroom window. He crawled down a nearby drainage ditch, scaled the wall surrounding a neighbor's house and cautiously edged his way to the rear of the convoy. He was able to commandeer a jeep and rush to the airport. Here he pulled rank and was flown to Semarang. Once back in Central Java he led the army garrison to remain loyal to the central Indonesian government.

During the next six weeks, a bloodbath took place in the country. Thousands of Indonesians were killed. Eyewitnesses said that the rivers were, at times, filled with floating bodies. Sarbini's troops held firm. The attempted coup failed. The country was saved.

In the decade following the quelling of the abortive Communist attempt at takeover, one of the great revivals of the twentieth century has taken place in Indonesia. Christians have had religious freedom as never before. Even though General Sarbini remains a Muslim, he has been warm to Christianity. Evangelicals have a friend in this governmental cabinet member.

The final pages of this story were only revealed to me a short time ago. The textbook used back in 1963 to teach General Sarbini conversational and written English was (as I'm sure you've surmised by now) the Gospel of John! How wonderful it must have been that day for the missionaries to hear him read, "In the beginning was the Word. and the Word was with God . . . and the Word was made flesh."

Music was used of God to touch the heart of a strategic general. A concert was God's means of opening a fast closed door. God's power was made manifest through song.

"Ask of me, and I will give thee the nations for thine inheritance, and the uttermost parts of the earth for thy possession."

Ask of Me . . . Jordan

I Walked Today Where Jesus Walked

Eastertide, 1967! Only weeks before the Six Day War. Jerusalem, the Holy City for Christians, Arabs, and Jews was experiencing its annual onslaught of visitors. Multitudes of Muslim pilgrims returning from Mecca by way of the Dome of the Rock elbowed their way past Christian shrines. It was Saturday before Easter Sunday.

Just off the mainstream of traffic on a quiet side street is the Garden Tomb—"The" Tomb—the grave which could not hold Christ. Preparations were being made for Easter services. Technicians were hanging amplifiers in ancient, gnarled olive trees. Dr. Mattar, the keeper of the Garden Tomb, was overseeing the moving of his precious German Steinway piano. Tenderly the workmen carried this prized possession to a rock ledge near the tomb. Tufts of Palestinian wild flowers gave splashes of color to the rocky soil.

My accompanist, Don Looser of Houston Baptist College, began to play. We rehearsed in preparation for our sacred concert scheduled for the Garden Tomb on Easter Sunday morning. How difficult it is to explain one's feelings while standing before the open Tomb and singing "Were you there when he rose up from the dead?" What a rare, unfathomable privilege!

Easter Sunday dawned. It was raining. Then sleet fell. It thundered! There was lightning! Finally, borne on gale winds, the stinging, engulfing, snow fell. A blizzard, the first in this century, struck Jerusalem. Traffic was paralyzed. Snow and mud slides closed major passes in the mountains of Jordan. Disappointment. Cancellation. No concert at Christ's Tomb. Was our trip to Jordan to be in vain? Why, Lord?

My Pathway Led Through Bethlehem

Kaleidoscopic pictures ever changing in intensity and patterns fell into place. The major thrust of our concert tour was not destined to be at the Tomb, but rather in rallies throughout Jordan. Don Looser and I experienced the joy of being instruments of his peace as we wandered down paths he knew. Our pathway led through Bethlehem. We "knelt, where all alone He prayed." As we traveled the length and breadth of this tiny nation, we sensed a oneness of fellowship with our Jordanian brothers in Christ. We were welcomed with a shalom of peace.

And Felt His Presence There

We sang unto the Lord and felt his presence there. Hundreds of Jordanians turned out for the concerts. Capacity crowds came to hear the gospel sung in Jerusalem, Amman, Ajloun, and other major centers of Baptist work in Jordan. The spirit evidenced by the audience in each place we performed was one of honest receptivity. The open opportunity to witness for Christ and his saving power in a Muslim land was unmistakable.

Unprecedented exposure was given to the Baptist cause when Don and I were interviewed over national radio. Of course, the government censors were there to cut out any material not acceptable for broadcast over the Jordanian network. But the amazing thing about the entire experience was the fact we were given freedom and much latitude in expressing our faith and our purpose for being in Jordan. The interviewer had us select some of our favorite classical numbers from the studio record library. They were played and then he asked us to comment on them. It was a real challenge to draw on some of our long forgotten music history data and musicological skills.

But the Lord seemed to use even this to speak to the emcee of the program. In the course of the interview, we both had ample opportunity to witness for Christ. Our Jerusalem concert was recorded in its entirety and rebroadcast over Radio Jordan. The scriptural continuity and testimony between each number were not cut. So through yet another medium of expression, the spoken word, we were allowed to witness.

Postlude

The Jordanian Baptist Evangelistic Crusade, which the concerts spearheaded, was blessed in an unusual way. In a period of one week the Baptist constituency of Jordan was more than doubled. Perhaps three hundred decisions for Christ does not sound phenomenal to us. Yet it really was miraculous. When one takes into account the fact that in Jordan when a profession of faith is made, the new convert becomes officially dead in the eyes of his family. He is openly persecuted, and in some instances his life is endangered.

Little did I realize when giving these concerts that this would perhaps be one of the last efforts of its kind in Jerusalem, Jordan. War clouds rolled over the country of Jordan in the early summer of 1967. The Arab and Jewish world had open conflict; the rest is history. The most productive part of Jordan, the West Bank, was taken by the victorious Israeli armies. I have often wondered what has happened to some of our new converts since this change in government. I wonder what happened to the jolly little Arab policeman who was a deacon in the Jerusalem Baptist Church, who so faithfully attended our concerts. Dr. Mattar, the keeper of the Garden Tomb, died during the six days of war. Three days after the battle began, he walked to his house from his hiding place in Christ's Tomb. He heard a knock at his gate and upon opening it was machine-gunned to death.

Many things remain a mystery to us, of course. One certainty does stand, however. Music does relate to people of other cultures. In an unusual way during Eastertide 1967, sacred concerts opened doors and attracted people to Baptist churches to hear the preached word. People came. People heard. People believed. "I will sing of the mercies of the Lord for ever: with my mouth will I make known my faithfulness to all generations" (Ps. 89:1).

Ask of Me . . . Africa

Kenya

My initial introduction to Africa was from thirty-five thousand feet. I awoke just as the blushing pink of dawn was suffusing the African bush. The Boeing jet was smoothly plying through the cloudless, equatorial skies.

After clearing customs at Nairobi, I was driven British style down the left-hand side of the road to the bougain-villea festooned Pan Afric Hotel. Here I had a lovely room with a balcony overlooking the capital city of Kenya. In the distance were ranges of mountains. Closer in were the rolling hills. A coolness belying our nearness to the Equator hovered over the mile high city. The smell of pungent eucalyptus smoke permeated the thin air. I slept for eighteen hours.

In the whirlwind activities of the next few days I with fresh eyes savored a country. It is always a revelation to see a country or continent for the very first time. Kenya provided termite hills over twenty feet tall; Kikuyu warriors plastered with cow dung and red ocher dye, carrying brightly painted shields and wicked looking spears; the Nairobi Game Preserve with its prides of lions, herds of zebras, cape buffalo, elephants, leopards, wild boars, antelope, gazelles, giraffes, wildebeests, and impala; native artisans carving ingenious artifacts from exotic tropical woods; native Christians whose testimonies of past persecution at the hands of the Mau Mau rival stories from *The Book of Martyrs.* How much has been paid by many of our Christian brothers in Africa to bear Christ's name.

Zambia

The prime network television program "Zambia at Seven" proved to be quite a happening. This program pulls one of the largest viewing audiences of any show in Zambia. My appearance coincided with the first week of microwave transmission for the Kitwe station to Lusaka. As the major news was coming on the air, there was a breakdown in communications between the two cities. A virtual holocaust of words broke loose. It reminded one of an old Charlie Chaplin movie. Technicians ran to and fro. Voices were raised to ultrasonic ranges. Yelling and bellowing via long-distance phone was the order of the day. Suddenly order reigned. "Zambia at Seven" came on at 7:14 P.M. The regular emcee became ill just moments before air time. The substitute sent to replace him was a major Zambian TV personality.

I sang several numbers at the beginning of the show. Then, in an unrehearsed dialogue, the emcee queried, "What are you doing in church music? Why aren't you in the entertainment field?" This led naturally to a Christian witness on my part and my calling to church music. Once again the emcee looked directly into the camera and said: "Dr. Rhea, you have spoken about a Christian experience. Tell me, just what is a Christian experience?"

The way was opened there on nationwide television to explain in very simple and cogent terms the gospel story. I suppose it was a moment I shall always remember. Never had there been any clearer indication of God's definite leadership in a particular situation. What a matchless joy to witness to the viewing audience of any entire nation! "Ask of me and I will give you the nations."

Ask of Me . . . Guatemala

Quezaltenango

Guatemala is a land of overpowering beauty. Rugged mountains pierce the deep blues of the cerulean skies. Variegated greens soften and relieve the lavish outpouring of nature's intense color scheme. Cities, villages, and open country alike provide *bas relief* to this colorful cyclorama.

Our journey from the capital to Quezaltenango, the second city of Guatemala, provided a spectacular introduction to this Central American nation. As we bounced

along in the mission's Volkswagen microbus, rapidly shifting and unfolding scenes of an ever-changing travelogue
vied for our attention. Spread round us in a vast hori-
zon-to-horizon "vista-vision" screen were breathtaking
scenarios—active volcanos belching out puffs of black
smoke; hairpin curves perched on dizzying precipices;
eerie, brushed-aside clouds which were shrouding sections
of rain-slick Pan-American highway; groaning intracity
diesel buses, heavily loaded with human cargo inside and
cooped chickens lashed onto luggage racks on topside.

My concert was held in the ornate nineteenth-century
opera house in Quezaltenango. Oval in shape, this building
is replete with gold leaf, gingerbread decor, crystal chan-
deliers, "diamond horseshoe" boxes, and red-velvet seats.
This historic house reflects the finest in transplanted European culture. At the appointed hour of 8:30 P.M. the Guatemalan national anthem was played. The crowd sang with
deep emotion. There was an enthusiastic response. Radio
Nacionale carried the full program both within the country
and by shortwave overseas. As I sang in an opera house
high in the mountains of Guatemala, my song could be
heard simultaneously around the world.

Later on that evening I retired to my room in a hotel
in downtown Quezaltenango. I was sleeping deeply. It must
have been about 3:00 A.M. With my "subconscious ears,"
I heard some extraordinary sounds. At first I thought it
was rain striking the tile roof. As I came to a fuller level
of awareness, I was certain it must be a woodpecker drilling
a metal gutter.

Then bolting upright in bed, I knew what it was—gunfire!
I smelled gunpowder. Round after round was being fired.
Even though I was on the second floor, I expected a stray,
wild shot might come coursing into my room at any moment. I threw myself onto the parquet floor and flattened

out against the bare, cold wood. Several hundred shots
were exchanged. Much excitement. Running in the court-
yard below. Yelling. The battle between the government
troops and the Cuban guerrilla infiltrators lasted for almost
an hour. Then an overt silence prevailed. After what
seemed to be an interminable wait, I felt it safe to peer
out the window. All was clear. I climbed back into bed.
My sweat-drenched body was chilled in the thin mountain
air. Sleep returned slowly.

Guatemala City

David Mein looked and acted like the Ambassador he
was. He and his charming wife warmly greeted Missionary
Clark Scanlon and his wife and me upon our arrival at
the American Embassy. The Ambassador was a product
of Baptist missionary parents. Reared in the Brazil Mission,
he felt perfectly at ease in Latin culture. His official lun-
cheon that day honored several visiting Americans. Among
the guests were Dr. and Mrs. Cameron Townsend, founders
of Wycliffe Bible Translators, and Arthur Morris, Board
Chairman of Rock City Packaging Company of Baltimore,
Maryland. It was a delightful occasion.

Served with all the style and pomp of a formal embassy
function, each guest was seated according to rigid protocol.
From my vantage point at the hostess's right, I could savor
the experience to the fullest. The servants were impeccably
trained. The damask-covered banquet table provided a
starch white backdrop for the gleaming service plates,
crested flatware, and translucent bone china embossed with
the Great Seal of the United States. Massive candelabra
held flickering candles. Their soft rays diffused delicately
from the silver water goblets. The waiters moved about
quietly and efficiently. Conversation was stimulating and
lively.

After lunch we went out onto the terrace for coffee. It had been raining and now the cool breezes were descending into the valley from the purple-hazed mountains. The embassy's manicured gardens were refreshed by the showers. Profusions of fragrant tropical flowers framed our view of the city and its environs.

Ambassador Mein requested that I sing for the guests. I accompanied myself on the fine Steinway grand piano in the drawing room. A brief prayer was led by Dr. Townsend. We all joined in singing "Blest Be the Tie That Binds."

As we were "saluted out" of the Embassy grounds by United States Marine guards, I reflected, "How wonderful to know that Americans have such an outstanding Christian as David Mein to represent us in this sensitive diplomatic post."

Less than a month later, Ambassador Mein and his native driver were mercilessly machine-gunned to death by terrorists on the streets of Guatemala City. "Precious in the sight of the Lord is the death of his saints."

Ask of Me . . . Philippines

Mindanao

Mindanao is one of the loveliest spots in the entire world. My introduction to this island was a memorable one. I bit down on a piece of Philippine Airline caramel candy. After two brief chews, out came one of my largest gold inlays. In that faraway place I didn't think it would be possible to have it securely cemented back into the "grand canyon" cavity in my lower right jaw. I soon learned that God takes care of those who are on mission for him. A wonderful Chinese Christian dentist by the unbelievable

name of Dr. Charlie Chan lived in Davao City on Mindanao. He replaced the inlay—without charge.

Because of the dental emergency, I was late for my
scheduled appearance for a radio interview in Davao City.
Arbie Montemayor, a local politician turned philan-
thropist, was the host of the talk show. He left word that
Missionary Howard Olive and I were to come to his home
for the taping session. We drove out to the outskirts of
the city. There nestled in the midst of a lovely coconut
palm grove was a walled estate. The guard opened the
gates, and we entered the long driveway overarched with
palm trees and flaming poincianas.

The architectural motif of the house was typical South
Sea island. We were ushered through great, open, airy
rooms. The trade winds provided any needed air-condi-
tioning. Breezes gently blew through the entire house. The
floors were white marble, the walls decorated with contem-
porary Philippine art.

We moved to a recording studio paneled in heavy mahogany. Mr. Montemayor came in to greet us, guided by
a companion. Our host was blind. He asked us to be seated.
Servants served us steaming hot coffee. He immediately
set me at ease and began the preinterview warm-up. He
told me about his blindness. I shared with him details of
my bout with cancer. We immediately communicated. Mr.
Montemayor had been a high official in the Philippine
government until his sudden blindness forced him to retire
from government service. He returned to Davao City and
entered into the business world. He prospered in copra
and real estate and became a millionaire many times over.

A beautiful, immediate rapport grew between us in those
moments. He signaled his engineer to "roll" the tape. Our
conversation ranged over many topics. Again and again
we touched upon things spiritual. We spoke of using one's

"gift" in God's service. Questions were posed about evangelical work in the Philippines—specifics regarding Baptist work that had never been asked before publicly on the media in that nation. At his insistence I shared my personal testimony.

The missionaries said later it was a first for Mindanao. For on the following day, Mr. Montemayor aired the entire interview—forty-five minutes in length. It was carried on the Inter-Island Network. The station manager estimated that over 500,000 persons listened that day.

Manila

Happy Birthday! What a way to spend one's forty-first. I was one of the guests at the state reception for then Vice-President (now President) William Tolbert of Liberia. The Baptist missionaries were invited by the protocol officer to help welcome this visiting Baptist VIP to the Philippines upon his arrival at the International Airport. This would be followed by our attendance at the state reception.

At the appointed hour we cleared security and entered the Airport VIP Lounge. Here we were briefed and given careful instructions on how to greet Vice-President Tolbert. At exactly 5:15 P.M., the Air France jet pulled up to the ramp. A contingent of Philippine Marines snapped to attention. The flags were waving. The band played. Dr. Tolbert stepped smartly from the plane. At the head of the stairs he was met by Vice-President Lopez of the Philippines and ceremoniously ushered down the long red carpet toward his waiting limousine. Each member of the diplomatic corps greeted him—the dean of the corps, American Ambassador G. Mennen Williams, the Liberian Ambassador, members of the consular corps. What fun it was to stand in the receiving line and observe first-hand the diplomatic amenities.

When Dr. Tolbert arrived in front of me, he stopped suddenly, broke into a wide, infectious grin, and said, "Claude, so good to see you again!" Much to my surprise he then reached over and gave me a big bear hug. The vice-president of the Philippines looked startled, then chuckled and effusively shook hands with me. Dr. Tolbert reminisced about our three-weeks journey together throughout Japan during the New Life Movement in 1963. He told me how pleased he was I would be leading the music for the Twelfth Baptist World Congress to be held in Tokyo in 1970.

He then rather reluctantly, it seemed, reverted into his official protocol-directed role as VIP. He stepped into the black Mercedes limousine and sped forward to a waiting President Marcos at the Presidential Palace. Vice-President Tolbert was protected both in front and behind the motorcade by jeep loads of machine gun armed guards. Motorcycles screamed and wailed like banshee vanguards. Happy Birthday!

Ask of Me . . . Japan

The Bullet

Bob Harper, art editor of *The Commission,* and I sauntered down the platform of the Osaka train station. What a sight we must have made in our French berets and travel-weary clothes. Bob was laden down with camera equipment. I was carrying music and a tattered suit bag stuffed with formal "black tails and white-tie" concert apparel. It was the end of the tour—almost. We clenched our reserved seat tickets in our teeth, bowed to the conductor, and were escorted down the aisle of the crack Japanese express train, *The Bullet.* This train was built for speed.

More than once it shattered all world speed records as it thundered down the rails in excess of 140 miles per hour between Osaka and Tokyo.

Bob Harper was on assignment to document and photograph my Far East concert tour for the Baptist Foreign Mission Board. What fun to travel with a creative artist and see countries through the eyes of a skilled painter/photographer.

We were the only Americans aboard *The Bullet* on that April evening. As we hurtled through the darkness of the Japanese countryside, Bob and I both sensed our foreignness to the situation. We sat surrounded by gaily chattering Japanese. They ate strange concoctions of rice and seaweed and overly ripe raw fish. Great quantities of green tea, Sappora brew and sake flowed. Occasionally they would nod to us and smile. Not one word of English was exchanged. All announcements over the public address system were made in rapid-fire Japanese.

According to our watches and the timetable provided by the travel agency, we were about one hour out of Tokyo. Without warning, the train came to a screeching, grinding stop. An announcement blared from the public address system. Looks of disbelief clouded the faces of our neighbors across the aisle. They furtively glanced at us and then once again retreated into their own thoughts.

We sat in a "spent" *Bullet* for almost two hours. Then slowly, deliberately, the train came to life. Once again the click of the wheels on the rails reassuringly lulled us to sleep.

I awoke with a start! *The Bullet* had stopped once again, as if in response to some unseen and foreboding emergency. The train seemed glued in place. once again the loudspeaker divested its terse announcement. Our Japanese train companions looked at Bob and me with real concern.

They seemed almost urgent in their glances.

Slowly, an old woman got up from her place. She mutely handed me a silk scarf. Through pantomime she indicated that I should place it over my head. A raincoat was placed around my shoulders. Bob was decked out in similar manner. A living phalanx of newfound friends surrounded us on all sides. Wonderingly we peered out over their heads and shoulders. The train crawled into Tokyo Station.

A nightmare scene greeted us. Broken windows. Smashed helmet liners. Debris strewn as far as I could see. Clouds of acrid tear gas floated sinuously above the nearly deserted platform. Then they appeared! Riot police in helmets and gas masks. The train stopped and at our very door was a protective cordon of Japanese troops.

One spoke in perfect English, apologizing for the condition of the station and explaining that student rioters, protesting American involvement in Okinawan affairs, had been on the rampage in the Ginza section of Tokyo all that evening. The police had learned by radio from *The Bullet* that two Americans were aboard. They feared that if our presence were discovered we would be attacked. The riot police escorted Bob and me to a waiting taxi. We were whisked at top speed to the safety of our hotel.

We shall long remember those gentle people on the train who were concerned for our safety and willingly were ready to become a living buffer against assault and attack.

Tokyo, 1970

The Herald Trumpeters of the Tokyo Symphony marched out on the balcony of the Budokan. Their long silver trumpets with velvet pendants attached gleamed in the July sunlight. Fanfare after fanfare burst upon the air.

The Twelfth Baptist World Congress was officially opened. Almost fifteen thousand Baptists from over fourscore nations streamed into the round assembly hall. Each delegate had gathered expectantly for this historic meeting.

I stood before the huge crowd and gave the downbeat. Thousands of voices in immediate concert raised paeons of praise. The one-hundred-piece symphony orchestra swelled the tune to almost unbearable beauty. The hall shook with myriads of tongues—so divergent—yet, so at one—"All hail the power of Jesus' name. Let angels prostrate fall. Bring forth the royal diadem and crown him Lord of all!"

Ask of Me . . . India

It was oppressively hot as Carolyn and I got off the plane in Bangalore. India's heat has a special quality. It's both prickly and moist. Even with inactivity I soon felt as if I were standing under a low-pressured shower—fully clothed—with tepid water slowly, but thoroughly saturating me. When the humid air is mixed with the din and assailing smells generated by the ever-present multitudes of people, the casual visitor to India is almost overwhelmed.

The missionaries welcomed us at the airport. They helped load our luggage into their van and then drove us into Bangalore. We bounced over the dusty road, scoring several near misses on the sacred cows. These animals have freedom to wander wherever they please. It is not at all uncommon to see them nudging pedestrians on sidewalks. In spite of widespread hunger on the part of the people, the Hindus still protect these cows as sacred objects and will not eat them. The Hindu religion sincerely embraces reincarnation. A cow might well be one's great grandfather.

Our hosts in India were the refreshing, unforgettable Hellingers. This outstanding surgeon and his family were making a significant impact on the city of Bangalore through their ministry both in the Baptist Out-Patient Clinic, and in field mission preaching stations. Dr. Hellinger invited me to give a concert at a small nearby settlement on the following Sunday morning.

This village was peopled by "untouchables." Even though the Constitution of India forbids caste, there was still a vestige of this cruel system left during the late 1960s. The people clustered in this makeshift collage of packing cases, scrap lumber, and temporary-type housing. As we entered the place, our nostrils were assaulted by a powerful stench. Hordes of little children ran out to greet us. Some had bloated bellies and the telltale red streaks of malnutrition at their hairline. Many were clothed in filthy rags. They reached out to us. Some hung onto our clothing. They were hungry—not only for food but also for love.

We picked our way through the refuse-strewn street until we stood before a small, bravely whitewashed little chapel. The roof was tin, the benches crude and rough. The floor was a mixture of dried mud and cow dung. We entered, opened the shutters, unfolded the portable pump organ we had been carrying, and made ready for worship services.

People began filling the chapel. They crowded in. They filled the benches, then sat on the floor. They stood at the windows. They blocked the doorway. The fierce Indian sun beat down upon the galvanized roof. The temperature rose inside to oven consistency. We sweltered and sweated and "stewed." Yet the intensity of the congregation's rapt attention captured and demanded our best. I have sung in many cathedrals around the world, but never have I experienced an hour of worship as meaningful as in that crude little Indian church house. I not only sang but simultaneously pumped the organ. It didn't take long for rivulets of perspiration to drench me completely. I sang and sweated. I testified to an audience over 90 percent of whom had never heard the gospel before.

We saw two Hindu women come to know the Lord Jesus Christ as Savior that day. Silently I prayed: *Thank you, God, for knowing the names of these "untouchables" and loving them enough to send your Son Christ Jesus to die for them.*

The next day, we experienced the other side of Indian culture, a command performance for the Maharaja and Maharani of Mysore State.

Several weeks earlier, engraved, embossed invitations had gone out to the "beautiful people" of that part of India, inviting them to attend a command performance by "the Dean of the School of Music at Samford University, Birmingham, Alabama, USA." The leading cultural, business, and governmental officials of Mysore State attended.

The Baptist Mission's beat-up Volkswagen brought us this time to a palace, not a village of the "untouchables." The grounds were neatly manicured. Fountains sparkled in the formal gardens. Peacocks strutted, displaying their irridescent plumage. A servant opened our car door and ushered us into the coolness of an Indian palace. Thick rugs covered the marble floors. Rich, opulent furniture was placed tastefully about the rooms. I was introduced to the guests by her majesty, the Maharani. The handmade German Bechstein piano was inlaid with silver. Its sound was delightful.

It was a tough audience—the president of Hindustani Airlines, the military commandant of that state, lovely ladies wearing brilliantly colored saris with solid gold threads running through them. Many of the women had diamonds adorning their noses. The red Brahman beauty mark was on their foreheads. A veneer of sophistication

and aloofness created a gulf between performer and audience. I tried every communication technique I had ever
learned in an attempt to break through their icy barrier.
   Nothing availed. Then I sang a simple Negro spiritual,
"He's Got the Whole World in His Hands." The children
of the royal family responded. They smiled and swayed
in rhythm to the music. They laughed in empathy when
I sang, "He's got the tiny little baby in His hand." Their
parents unbent. Smiles broke out. The gospel in song was
finding lodging in hearts that had never before heard. I
prayed gratefully: *Thank you God for knowing the names
of these "up and outs," these rulers of India. Thank you
for giving your Son for them.*
   The thought kept coming to me again and again.
Whether you're a Maharaja or an "untouchable," or somewhere in between, you still have need for a Savior. The
sovereign God who holds the whole world in his hand
has made a way for each of us to come back into full
fellowship with himself. That way, the only way, is through
Jesus Christ, God's only begotten Son!

The Power of Music

   In the August 1969, issue of the Baptist world mission
journal, *The Commission,* Leland Webb wrote an article
entitled "The Power of Music." He summarized the thrust
and scope of my musical missionary efforts. Excerpts from
his writing are quoted as a closing section of "Ask of Me."

   They came individually and in groups. At the door
   they presented their copies of the printed circular that
   served as admission tickets.
      Each person took a pencil and a card listing Chris-

tian decisions. By the dozens they came until the
supply of pencils ran short, and the Korean Baptists
at the door began breaking them in half to double
the number.

By the hundreds they came until there was standing
room only on this rainy Sunday afternoon in Taejon,
Korea. They kept coming until some 1,200 were gathered in the Methodist high school auditorium that
served as concert hall.

It was the opening rally for the 1970 Baptist evangelistic crusades in Korea. The invitation circulars had
been distributed selectively, so most of those present
were not Christians.

Music had brought them together. They had not
come through the rain to hear a Christian testimony
but to hear a concert by a visiting tenor from America.

They applauded expectantly when the American
was introduced. In stocking feet (shoes are barred
because of the floor finish) he strode on stage and
began with "How Great Thou Art." As he repeated
the chorus, the Korean audience gasped when they
realized he was singing this chorus in their language.

The singer's sincerity and warmth reached across
the footlights, beyond culture and language. The audience was his.

Claude H. Rhea, Jr., had begun another Christian
concert, his first in Korea. . . . The concert lasted
about two hours. A Korean soprano and Mrs. Frank
L. Baker, a missionary associate, also a soprano, sang
during intermission.

But the afternoon did not end with Rhea's last
selection. Through an interpreter he gave an invitation
to accept Christ as Savior, explaining each of the
spiritual choices listed on the cards the audience had

received. Each listener was invited to check any commitment and to leave the card at his seat.

Later the cards were collected. Out of the 1,200
persons present, more than 500 indicated they would
welcome a visit from a Baptist church to bring infor-
mation about the Christian faith, and provided their
addresses; 53 expressed interest in accepting Christ
as Savior; 37 made professions of faith in Christ.

All of them had been drawn to hear the gospel
by a concert.

The afternoon was not yet over. The concert had
been jointly sponsored by Baptists and by the local
newspaper (which added prestige to the event). Immediately after the performance, a group of reporters,
university faculty members, and students—some 50
persons in all—met Rhea at a press conference.

Held over tea, the conference started sedately
enough. Then a professor asked, "What are some of
the different ways of teaching singing in parts?" The
conference became a sing-in.

"One way," said Rhea, "is to begin by singing in
rounds." He divided the gathering into three groups,
one to sing "Row, Row, Row Your Boat," another
"Three Blind Mice," and the third "Are You Sleeping
Brother John?" These words were English but everyone joined in.

That night Rhea presented a concert at a local
Baptist church. The sounds of sirens were heard over
the music as a fire raged in the city's main market.
Numbers of small businesses were burned out. In a
moving moment, Rhea paused for special prayer for
the fire's victims.

The next evening Rhea was in Seoul, the capital,
for a concert to a capacity crowd in the National

Theater, sponsored by the Korean Baptist Convention in connection with the 1970 crusade.

A controversy over prayer delayed the start. A rule states that no Christian can voice public prayer in the National Theater. The concert finally began. For his closing number, Rhea *sang* a prayer.

Before leaving the country, Rhea was soloist at the Korean Baptist Convention meeting. During less than four days in the country, he had directed the thinking of many individuals toward the gospel, made friends for the Christian cause, and helped arouse interest in Baptist evangelistic plans. . . .

The persuasion of music in finding the way to a man's soul through his ears is illustrated in memories Rhea has stored up during these years:

—Being tenor soloist for the performance of Mendelssohn's *Elijah* in Recife, Brazil, the first performance anywhere in Portuguese, so far as is known;

—Hearing the cries of "Encore!" by an enthusiastic, whistling, foot-stomping audience in Santiago, Chile.

—Facing a noisy audience of boys at the national (Brazilian) Royal Ambassador congress in Rio de Janeiro, Brazil, inquiring as to the Portuguese word for "quiet," and securing a hush by singing in a prolonged tone, "SILENCIO!"

—Giving a benefit concert, sponsored by Hong Kong Baptist Association, to help send refugee children to summer church camp, and faltering while rendering "Turn Your Eyes Upon Jesus" when confronted by the unseeing eyes of a group of blind refugee children.

Some memories illustrate how things seem to work out against obstacles. For instance, purchase of radio and television time for a Christian concert in a strongly Muslim city in Malaysia was at first described as impossible. But then Rhea was given permission to sing on the air, using only classical music.

The program director asked to see the music Rhea was to use. Handing him the classical numbers for examination, Rhea kept shuffling through other music.

"Is this all you have?" asked the director, as Joseph Underwood related it in his book *By Love Compelled.*

"No," replied Rhea. "I have some other music here that I consider to be better and which I would rather sing, but it is Christian music."

The director looked it over and saw its quality. "Since Sunday is Easter," he said finally, "we will let you sing all sacred music if that is what you wish to do."

"So," concluded Underwood, "in the city where many scoff at the idea of the resurrection of Jesus Christ, for the first time in history, by television and radio, the resurrection victory of Jesus Christ was announced." . . . Such is the force of music as evidenced in the ministry of one man.

"Ask of me, and I will give thee the nations for thine inheritance and the uttermost parts of the world for thy possession" (Ps. 2:8).

With My Song I Will Praise Him

"So Send I You"

So send I you, to take to souls in bondage
 The word of truth that sets the captive free,
To break the bonds of sin, to loose death's fetters,

So send I you, to bring the lost to me.

"As the Father hath sent me,
So send I you." [1]*

—E. MARGARET CLARKSON

8 A Man's Gift Brings Him Before Great Men

"[A man's gift] brings him before great men" (Prov. 18:16, RSV).

Proverbs 18:16 contains a double-barreled blessing. Not only does this Scripture share the promise that our gift or talent will make room for us but it also assures us that if we use our endowment for God, he will bless us by multiplying the effectiveness of the gift manyfold and by bringing us before great men. We will stand there as equals. Liberated. Channels of his love. Freed to testify that we are heirs to and recipients of God's limitless reservoir of goodness, blessings, and grace gifts. I am convinced that Proverbs 18:16 is one of God's formulas for attaining higher happiness along the pilgrimage.

Deo Fisus Labora

During my undergraduate days at William Jewell College, I was confronted many times with the school's motto *Deo Fisus Labora.* It was printed on the school's logo, on the great seal, on the stationery, and even inscribed on the front of the chapel. I was a student for over two years before I took the trouble to translate the motto into English. *Deo Fisus Labora*—"Trust in God and Work." What potent

135

words!

Upon initial examination, this statement, "Trust in God and Work," seems somewhat contradictory. If one trusts God enough, why bother with the activism of work? Contained within this seemingly variant statement lies a realistic gem of truth. Herein is found a valid formula—TRUST PLUS WORK YIELDS ACHIEVEMENT. *Deo Fisus Labora* teamed with Proverbs 18:16 is an equation which can serve as an important foundation stone for building a productive life. I have found it to be an equation that balances.

Deo Fisus (Trust in God)

Inherent in the word *trust* is faith. "Faithing" God is fascinating. It thrusts aside man-made, self-imposed limitations. Faith is not for vocation alone but also for permeation into *every* facet of living. Trust in God is an adventure. Faith in God is an unseen map for guiding us through days of preparation and throughout each common, human venture. I have discovered that faith tested yields validity and becomes a vital ingredient in life itself.

Labora (Work)

The second component of the achievement equation is work. One does not commit his gifts and talents to a beneficent God and then sit idly back and wait for things to happen. A continuous process of self-evaluation must be undertaken. A perseverance and tenacity of purpose must be developed. Performance which is worthy is an outgrowth of these factors. Trust in God *and* work! All too frequently we are prone to lean contentedly upon the everlasting arms of "trust" and not make any intelligent efforts to put feet under our dreams. Work in its pure, unadulterated form is a most necessary catalyst for precipitating achievement.

In my continuing quest of faith and work, I have found three valuable guideposts for structuring my thought and actions: perspective, perseverance, and performance.

Perspective

If you would use the gift which God has given you, it would be wise to take an honest look at yourself. Just what *has* God given you? To find out, use your own common sense; utilize vocational guidance techniques. Determine what your gifts and talents really are. Face up to yourself; accept yourself. There will never be another you, for you are unique; you have a mission to fulfill. Dare to think great and noble thoughts as to your destiny. Set worthy goals. Subjugate selfishness; nurture love; deepen the roots of faith. Adjust the telescope of perspective until you can see clearly defined images of your goals.

Perseverance

A second guidepost is perseverance. Perseverance is a dogged determination that nothing will stop you from achieving your God-directed goals. Perspiration—yes! Stick-to-itiveness—yes! All this and more. Perseverance is the drive which will not allow you to give in to the menace of mediocrity. It is the surge of productivity which causes you to develop and polish your gift. Perseverance is the burning desire to interpret and execute the Creator's blueprint of your life and to erect the structure which the divine Architect foresaw. In short, perseverance is work.

Performance

The end result of perspective and perseverance is the actual performance of one's task. Herein work continues, for we must seek diligently to make each day's performance worthy in the sight of God. We must never be content with past achievements but should ever be alert to press forward to new frontiers and opportunities for performance of still undetermined and unfathomed tasks. Trust in God and work.

Standing Before Great Men

As I have sought to use my gift to His honor, I have stood before many great men of my generation—Christian statesmen, a president of the United States, political, diplomatic, business, governmental and cultural leaders of the world. I have stood before them as an equal and witnessed.

One such interesting opportunity came when the mayor of Houston, Texas, appointed me Houston's "Singing Ambassador to the Orient." Armed with scrolls of honorary citizenship and with gold keys to the city of Houston, I conferred Texas status upon major leaders of Southeast Asia. Doors were opened for missionaries to accompany me into these series of ceremonies.

An especially strategic contact was made with the Prime Minister of Thailand, Field Marshall Kittakachorn. A twenty-minute audience was granted. A few minutes before the appointed hour, Missionary Ronald Hill and I presented our credentials to the guard at the door of the imposing, palatial governmental building. We were admitted to an anteroom and asked to be seated. At 2:00 the double doors were opened by liveried attendants, the protocol officer strode toward us and beckoned us to follow

him. We were led into the audience room of an Oriental
potentate. Thick, opulent rugs engulfed our feet. Gold
embroidered tapestries hung on the teak paneled walls.
Thai brass highlighted the room's decor. Incongruently,
at the far end of the room was a Louis the Fifteenth antique
couch. Huge elephant tusks stood at each end of the couch.
Behind on the wall hung a garish oil painting of an elephant.   Prime Minister Kittakachorn and his retinue stood
midway down the red carpet. The protocol officer made
the official introductions. Missionary Hill interpreted. The
ceremony began. I presented the Prime Minister with the
scroll and gold key and "by the power invested in me
by the city of Houston," made him an honorary Texan.
He smiled broadly and accepted the accolade.

I then asked the protocol officer for a point of personal
privilege. He granted me this, and I presented the Prime
Minister one of my vocal recordings, *Majestic Themes*.
Once again the Prime Minister smiled broadly and accepted the gift. I then asked if he would accept a final
gift I had brought him. Through the interpreter he indicated that he would. I then said, "Mr. Prime Minister,
on behalf of some three thousand evangelical Christians
in Thailand, I am indeed happy to present you a copy
of the Bible, God's Word, written in the Thai language."
The Prime Minister accepted the Bible. The television
cameras whirred. The event was documented for viewing
on the national network.

Then, much to our surprise and the apparent chagrin
of the protocol officer who was responsible for keeping
the appointment schedule running on time, the Prime
Minister asked me to be seated. We had a delightful visit
there on that antique French sofa. The conversation ranged
from international affairs to sights to be sure to see in
Thailand. Before leaving, I had the chance to tell him about

my Christian faith. As we were escorted out of the audience room, I could not help but reflect once again on the promise, "A man's gift makes room for him and brings him before great men."

Achievement

In 1961, William Jewell College honored me with a *Citation for Achievement.* Each year several alumni are invited to return to the campus and present their philosophy of life to the assembled student body. A speaker of national significance is featured in the morning convocation. Vice-President Lyndon B. Johnson spoke that year.

As an honored alumnus, I was asked to present briefly my concept and definition of achievement. In the final paragraphs of my talk. I shared the following thoughts with the students:

> Today I've been called back to my Alma Mater to be honored as one who has "achieved." Could it be the formula has worked? Has the cycle which began in 1948 during a Focus Week here at William Jewell been completed? No, it is not finished. I have no illusions of grandeur. I have not yet fully "achieved." But of this I am confident. God's promise has proved true—"A man's gift maketh room for him and bringeth him before great men." As I have sought to use my "gift" to His honor, I have stood before greats. Yet, I must honestly pose one more series of related questions. Who are these great men? What is greatness? What *is* achievement? Is it public acclaim? Honor? Status? Title? Wealth? Political prestige?

"Only God's microscope discerns true greatness. Its lens brings into sharp focus one's total life. The deeds accomplished are seen within the context of one's heart, and the purposes which prompted them are laid bare.

"That life is magnified which seeks humbly to serve as God's communication upon earth, sharing with mankind the blessing of God's knowledge, wisdom, compassion and love. Thus a man's own identity is merged with the greatness of God—outside of which, isolated human achievement is dwarfed to insignificance." [1]

Afterglow

That same November evening, a roster of distinguished guests prepared to enter the Muehlbach Hotel in Kansas City for the Achievement Day Dinner. Suddenly, without warning, a fire broke out in the hotel kitchen. Smoke billowed out. Fire engines screamed to the scene. Hoses stretched in crazy spaghetti-like patterns on the street. Former President Harry S Truman and other VIPs in black-tie outfits and formal gowns, nimbly stepped over fire-fighting equipment and tiptoed through puddles of water. The dinner steaks were more than well done! Disappointment. Public relations' nightmare! The banquet cancelled. The F.B.I. rushed Lyndon B. Johnson back to his waiting plane.

Later on as we sat in our room reviewing the events of that memorable day, my wife Carolyn chuckled and made a wise observation. "Darling," she mused, "this just proves one thing—the fleetingness of human achievement." How true her words! Oswald Chambers put it another way when he said, "The test of the life of a saint is not success but faithfulness in human life as it actually is." *Deo fisus labora.* "Trust in God and Work." And, I dare you—claim and appropriate Proverbs 18:16 for your life. It works!

With My Song I Will Praise Him

"Thine, Lord"

Thine, Lord, only Thine,
Thine, Lord, only Thine,
Take me, use me as Thou wilt, dear Saviour,
Thine, Lord, only Thine,
Thine, Lord, only Thine.

—ROBERT HARKNESS

9 The Great American Dream

*"But seek ye first the kingdom of God, and his righteousness;
and all these things shall be added unto you" (Matt. 6:33).*

I've never been really sure what the "great American
dream" is. Those of us who came through college during
post-World War II days were automatically heirs to an
emerging, materialistic, gray-flannel suit brand of success.
It seemed that our nation's highest priority was the
achievement of wealth for one's self no matter what it
cost the next guy. You know the formula as well as I:
the home in suburbia, the cars and color television sets,
the scrubbed children, "keeping up with (and surpassing)
the Joneses," the weekends around the barbecue at the
lake house, or behind the power mower. "The standard
American package," Harvard sociologist David Riesman
calls it.

Now almost a generation beyond 1945, the postwar
dream loses luster. The freeways have carved our land.
Pollution has enveloped our cities. Unwise exploitation of
our natural resources has depleted our national riches.

As breadwinner and provider for his household, the
American male has, by and large, been unable to escape
from the insidious pressures ever-increasingly placed upon
him by the "system" to procure more and better "things"
for his loved ones. It is easy for the head of the household

to get caught up in a substitution of material objects for substantive intrinsics.

It was during my very personal experiment with and pursuit of the "standard American package" that I gleaned hard-learned lessons—both about myself and about one who took unfair advantage of me.

It all started during a brainstorming session. Three partners logically questioned, "Why not put electronic pianos inside school buses, drive these mobile music laboratories to rural areas, and provide much-needed musical training for culturally deprived children?" The rationale seemed so sound. The ingredients were all there. The trained teachers were available. The school administrators were cooperative. The market of student potential was vast. Projections were run. They turned out positively.

So we incorporated to meet an obvious need—and in the best American tradition of private enterprise, to make a profit. A leasing firm was also organized. This company purchased and renovated the buses and secured the needed piano laboratories. Substantial financing was sought and obtained. As corporate officers, I and another person signed the necessary papers. We pledged our good names and risked material resources to back the venture.

Over fifteen hundred students were initially recruited to study in the mobile piano laboratories. Registration fees were paid. Monthly payment plans were begun. The money began to flood into the home office in the northern part of the state—or so the computer printout showed. The income ran beyond projections. A handsome profit was accruing. The buses ran. The pianos were played. The payments to the lending agency were promptly paid. Two months passed, then three. The concept was a success. The company was making it!

Then came December—bleak December. The teachers

complained and then threatened to sue. My partner had not paid them fully for November. The due date came and then passed for the monthly installment to be paid on the equipment. I was told that "things were a bit tight but would straighten out in a few weeks." I visited the lending agency and reassured them. January. February. Retrenchment. No more bothering to send me "doctored" financial reports. Phone calls unanswered. Personal relationships ruptured. Misappropriation and gross mismanagement on the part of one whom I had trusted. Flight from the state and finally from the country by my partner. I was left holding the proverbial "bag." My name was on the note with his—but he had chosen to abandon the floundering project.

It was a lonely, trying time personally. I was wiped out financially. There was nothing left but five school buses, twenty electric pianos, and rapidly escalating "past-due" interest and principal payments. Liquidation. Refinancing. Reduction in our family financial outlay. A lonely climb from the darkness of engulfing debt to blessed surcease near the end of the tunnel.

I had avidly pursued the "great American dream" and its hoped-for rewards. It had soured. Through blind faith in one whom I trusted implicitly, I had helped spawn a failure. What had gone awry? Hadn't my motivation to serve deserving young people been noble enough in concept? What's wrong with making a profit? Is it a sin to succeed materially? I rationalized my position. Materialism is certainly not the highest good, but its emoluments are attractive and can be used for good.

As it turned out, the good life promised in the pursuit of the "great American dream" not only wasn't personally rewarding to me—it was hardly palatable. What then should be my response as His disciple to this set of circumstances? Can I participate in marketplace activities and still retain my posture as a Christian? What is my role during those days when failure stalks my path and I am experiencing the discipline of difficulty?

I'm not certain I have complete answers yet. I have come to believe, however, that at least two redemptive lessons were taught me during this financial crisis.

Lesson 1: God gives us life as we overcome.

God does not give us overcoming life. He gives us life as we overcome. The strain is the strength. If there is no strain, there is no strength . . . God never gives strength for tomorrow, or for the next hour; but for the strain of the minute. The temptation is to face difficulties from a common-sense standpoint. The saint is hilarious when he is crushed with difficulties because the thing is so ludicrously impossible to anyone but God.[1]

Lesson 2: Christians should not look for justice in this world.

Jesus indicates in the Sermon on the Mount that as his followers there are times when we will not be dealt with justly. Christians should never look for justice in this world, yet we should never cease to give it.

How difficult to forgive when our pocketbook has been wronged. It is hard not to feel vindictive against one who takes advantage of us, wreaks havoc on our well-laid financial plans, and raids irreparably our future security.

Our true hope cannot be in dreams built upon foundations of sand. Inevitably it seems that it is during those times when we enthrone our own common sense and lean to our own understanding that we are most in danger of failure. Only as we abdicate and let him fill every facet of our being can our dreams be built upon a solid foundation. God is like a refiner's fire, whose white heat consumes the dross and makes pure our motives.

The words of our Lord still supercede with priority and urgency any "great American dream"—"Seek ye first the kingdom of God, and his righteousness; and all these things shall be added unto you."

With My Song I Will Praise Him

"The New Twenty-Third"

Because the Lord is my Shepherd
I have everything that I need
He lets me rest in meadows green
and leads me beside the quiet stream.
He keeps on giving life to me
And helps me to do what honors Him the most.
Even when walking through the dark valley of death,
I will never be afraid
For He is close beside me
Guarding, guiding all the way
He spreads a feast before me in the presence of mine
    enemies.

*By Ralph Carmichael. Copyright 1969, Lexicon Music, Inc. Woodland Hills CA 91364.
All rights reserved. Used by permission.

10 What God Hath Promised

"And being fully persuaded that, what he had promised, he was able also to perform" (Rom. 4:21).

On these pages, I have attempted to be transparent and to share openly with you some happenings that have transpired in my life. You have read of my joys and sorrows. You have experienced with me moments of testing and triumph. You have felt my heartaches as well as celebrations.

I hope that these personal recountings have shed some light on your own pilgrimage. My intent has been to communicate that every human being is subject both to buffeting trials and occasional success. We should not think it strange when we are caught in the throes of some seemingly inescapable human milieu. We are not alone in being heir to these common ventures of life. What one of us has not had those futile times when nothing made sense? Each one of us has questioned the very *why* of living.

Yet, conversely, we have tasted moments of high ecstasy when we've been possessed with the certain conviction that we are indeed children of God!

Life is never a straight line. It has its jagged ups and downs. As his followers, however, we can live and move and have our being in God. We are kept under the covert of his undergirding, overarching, all encompassing promises.

149

150

 WITH MY SONG I WILL PRAISE HIM

God Hath Promised . . . Strength for the Day
* "But they that wait upon the Lord shall renew their strength; they shall mount up with wings as eagles; they shall run and not be weary; and they shall walk, and not faint" (Isa. 40:31).
* "The Lord is good, a strong hold in the day of trouble; and he knoweth them that trust in him" (Nah. 1:7).
* "That he would grant you, according to the riches of his glory, to be strengthened with might by his spirit in the inner man" (Eph. 3:16).
"For my strength is made perfect in weakness" (2 Cor. 12:9).

God Hath Promised . . . Rest for the Labor
* "Come unto me, all ye that labour and are heavy laden, and I will give you rest" (Matt. 11:28).
* "The Lord thy God in the midst of thee is mighty; he will save, he will rejoice over thee with joy; he will rest in his love, he will joy over thee with singing" (Zeph. 3:17).

God Hath Promised . . . Light for the Way
* "I am the light of the world: he that followeth me shall not walk in darkness, but shall have the light of life" (John 8:12).
* "Thy word is a lamp unto my feet, and a light unto my path" (Ps. 119:105).
* "The entrance of thy words giveth light; it giveth understanding unto the simple" (Ps. 119:130).
* "The Lord is my light and my salvation; whom shall I fear?" (Ps. 27:1).
* "If we walk in the light, as he is in the light, we have fellowship one with another, and the blood of Jesus Christ his Son cleanseth us from all sin" (1 John 1:7).

* "For God, who commanded the light to shine out of darkness, hath shined in our hearts, to give the light of the knowledge of the glory of God in the face of Jesus Christ" (2 Cor. 4:6).

God Hath Promised . . . Grace for the Trials
* "My grace is sufficient for thee" (2 Cor. 12:9).
* "For the Lord God is a sun and shield: the Lord will give thee grace and glory: no good thing will he withhold from them that walk uprightly" (Ps. 84:11).
* "But he giveth more grace. Wherefore he saith, God resisteth the proud, but giveth grace unto the humble" (Jas. 4:6).

God Hath Promised . . . Helps from Above
* "Many are the afflictions of the righteous; but the Lord delivereth him out of them all" (Ps. 34:19).
* "When thou passeth through the waters, I will be with thee; and through the rivers, they shall not overflow thee: when thou walkest through the fire, thou shalt not be burned; neither shall the flame kindle upon thee" (Isa. 43:2).
* "And we know that all things work together for good to them that love God, to them who are the called according to his purpose" (Rom. 8:28).

God Hath Promised . . . Unfailing Sympathy
* "The Lord is merciful and gracious, slow to anger, and plenteous in mercy" (Ps. 103:8).
* "Like as a father pitieth his children, so the Lord pitieth them that fear him. For he knoweth our frame; he remembereth that we are dust" (Ps. 103:13-14).
* "It is of the Lord's mercies that we are not consumed, because his compassions fail not" (Lam. 3:22).

God Hath Promised . . . Undying Love

* "Yea, I have loved thee with an everlasting love: therefore with lovingkindness have I drawn thee" (Jer. 31:3).

* "But God commendeth his love toward us, in that, while we were yet sinners, Christ died for us" (Rom. 5:8).

* "Herein is love, not that we loved God, but that he loved us, and sent his Son to be the propitiation for our sins" (1 John 4:10).

* "Who shall separate us from the love of Christ? shall tribulation, or distress, or persecution, or famine, or nakedness, or peril, or sword? Nay, in all these things we are more than conquerors through him that loved us" (Rom. 8:35, 37).

* "Finally, brethren, farewell. Be perfect, be of good comfort, be of one mind, live in peace; and the God of love and peace shall be with you" (2 Cor. 13:11).

With My Song I Will Praise Him

"What God Hath Promised"

God hath not promised skies always blue,
Flower-strewn pathways all our lives through;
God hath not promised sun without rain,
Joy without sorrow, peace without pain.
But God hath promised strength for the day,
Rest for the labor, light for the way,
Grace for the trials, help from above,
Unfailing sympathy, undying love.

—ANNIE JOHNSON FLINT

POSTLUDE

God's grace gifts await our appropriation. Rise then. Accept them. Serve him. Love him. Live abundantly. Give God the glory! With *your* song praise him!

"The Lord is my defense and my shield; my heart trusteth in Him, and I am helped. Therefore my heart rejoices, and with my song I will praise him" (Ps. 28:7, Berkeley).

NOTES

Chapter 1

1. Carolyn Rhea, *My Heart Kneels, Too* (New York: Grosset & Dunlap, Inc.). Used by permission.
2. Audrey Mieir, "Don't Spare Me, Lord." © Copyright 1959 by Manna Music, Inc., 2111 Kenmere Ave., Burbank, CA 91504. International Copyright Secured. All Rights Reserved. Used by Permission.

Chapter 2

1. "Precious Lord, Take My Hand," by Thomas Dorsey. Copyright 1938 by Chappell Music Co. All rights reserved. Used by permission.

Chapter 3

1. Oswald Chambers, *My Utmost for His Highest* (New York: Dodd, Mead & Co., 1935), p. 243. Used by permission.

Chapter 5

1. Carolyn Rhea, *Such Is My Confidence* (New York: Grosset & Dunlap, Inc., 1961). Used by permission.
2. Adapted from a forthcoming book by Carolyn Rhea to be published by Zondervan Publishing House, Grand Rapids, Michigan.
3. Chambers, op. cit., p. 129.

4. © 1975 by Lillenas Publishing Co. All rights reserved. Used by permission.

Chapter 6

1. *Such Is My Confidence,* op. cit., p. 76.

Chapter 7

1. Copyright 1954 by Singspiration, Inc. All rights reserved. Used by permission.

Chapter 8

1. Rhea, *Such Is My Confidence,* op. cit.

Chapter 9

1. Chambers, op. cit., p. 215.
2. By Ralph Carmichael. Copyright 1969, Lexicon Music, Inc. Woodland Hills, CA 91364. All rights reserved. Used by permission.